MIRRORS and WINDOWS
镜子与窗户

East-West Poems with translations
中西诗译诗选

ESSENTIAL ANTHOLOGIES SERIES 14

Guernica Editions Inc. acknowledges the support of
the Canada Council for the Arts and the Ontario Arts Council.
The Ontario Arts Council is an agency of the Government of Ontario.
We acknowledge the financial support of the Government of Canada

MIRRORS and WINDOWS
镜子与窗户

East-West Poems with translations
中西诗译诗选

Translated, Compiled and Edited by
ANNA YIN

GUERNICA
EDITIONS
TORONTO · CHICAGO · BUFFALO · LANCASTER (U.K.)
2021

Michael Mirolla & Connie McParland, general editors
Anna Yin, editor
Cover and interior design: Rafael Chimicatti
Guernica Editions Inc.
287 Templemead Drive, Hamilton (ON), Canada L8W 2W4
2250 Military Road, Tonawanda, N.Y. 14150-6000 U.S.A.
www.guernicaeditions.com

Distributors:
Independent Publishers Group (IPG)
600 North Pulaski Road, Chicago IL 60624
University of Toronto Press Distribution (UTP)
5201 Dufferin Street, Toronto (ON), Canada M3H 5T8
Gazelle Book Services, White Cross Mills
High Town, Lancaster LA1 4XS U.K.

First edition.
Printed in Canada.

Legal Deposit – Third Quarter
Library of Congress Catalog Card Number: 2021935733
Library and Archives Canada Cataloguing in Publication
Title: Mirrors and windows : East-West poems with translations = Jing zi yu chuang
hu : zhong xi shi yi shi xuan / translated, compiled and edited by Anna Yin.
Other titles: Mirrors and windows (Guernica) | Jing zi yu chuang hu
Container of (work): Mirrors and windows (Guernica) | Container of (expression):
Mirrors and windows (Guernica). Chinese Names: Yin, Anna, translator, editor.
Description: Series statement: Essential anthologies ; series 14
Poems in English and Chinese, translated from the English.
Identifiers: Canadiana 20210140127 | ISBN 9781771836159 (softcover) Subjects:
LCSH: Canadian poetry—21st century. | LCSH: Canadian poetry—21st century—
Translations into Chinese. | CSH: Canadian poetry (English)—21st century.
CSH: Canadian poetry (English)—21st century—Translations into Chinese.
Classification: LCC PS8099.C5 M57 2021 | DDC C811/.608—dc23

CONTENTS

Part 2: From Chinese to English | 中诗英译

Part 3: Poems Inspired by translations| 译者之意外收获

Mirrors and Windows

In this mirror,
I draw the heart
in subtle red,
ripe with the paradise fruit ...
Our dream rises with its light.

Follow me and enter
the deep dazzling dark:
in each bloom,
we find—the eye (i)
sees through windows.

In 1967, U.S. Country & Western singer George Jones issued a tune whose refrain swore, "If my heart had windows, / Use yours for love just for you." The idea was, the male lover would be able to enjoy vicariously the female's love, even if it were only for herself. In other words, his heart would be able to translate her self-love into a shared love. I think that the translation of poetry works similarly: One peers lovingly—even squints upon—the original work, and then seeks out equivalently fresh, equally true, meanings in the diction of the receiving or importing language.

But I imagine that a similar process occurs in writing any poem —even in one's native tongue, for each poem is a translation of inspiration, of lived experience, of the whole language distilled into one set of terms. My own mother-tongue, English, is itself always in the midst of translation—evolution and devolution— having originated as a mishmash of Anglo-Saxon-Germanic-Norse grunts and growls (sounded while were dudes spearing bears or clubbing down boars) plus the courtly, diplomatic *suavité* of the Norman French, plus the polysyllabic Latin of the Catholic monasteries, so ideal for euphemism, legalism, and abstraction. Thus, when I come to write a poem—ostensibly in English—I'm echoing its origins in my diction, in my mix of monosyllables and polysyllables, and then *via* the lingoes (plural) specific to me as an African-Canadian, born and raised among the Bluenosers (in Nova Scotia), but of African-American (partial) roots. Thus, my poetry "translates" English into Canadian, Ebonics, Nova Scotian, and even shards of French (an official language in Canada), plus the academic diction in which I'm steeped as a scholar ....

美国著名乡村音乐歌手乔治·琼斯在1967年发行的一首歌中唱到，"如果我心有窗，/用你的爱，爱只为你。"意思是，男方可以爱女方所爱，即使这爱只是为女方自己。换句话说，他的心能够将她的所爱转化为共同的爱。我认为诗歌翻译也是异曲同工：译者欣喜地端详——甚至眯着眼睛——凑近原作，然后在合适的语言的言辞里寻找同等新鲜，同样真实的含义。

但我想，在写一首诗时也会出现类似的过程——即使是用一种本地语言，因为每首诗都是灵感，生命体验，整个语言被净化成一组术语的翻译。我自己的母语，英语，本身总是处于翻译——进化和流传中——起源于盎格鲁-撒克逊-日耳曼-挪威语的咕噜声和咆哮声（听起来像勇士猎熊或者追捕豪猪）再加上诺尔曼法语的宫廷，外交，以及天主教的多音节拉丁语，非常适合委婉的措辞，立法和抽象。因此，当我来写一首诗——表面在用英文——实际上我在回应它的起源，在单音节和多音节的混合中追溯我作为非洲裔加拿大人所特有的语言，以及出生在新斯科舍省的非裔美洲人（部分）根源。因此，我写诗时是将英语翻译成加拿大语，黑檀语，新斯科舍语，甚至是法语（另一加拿大官方语言），并加上我作为学者浸染的学术用语。

同样，不可避免地，现代英语翻译都拜托先辈美国现代主义诗人埃兹拉.庞德，他重塑英语诗歌——"力求新颖"——借鉴了中国，法国（普罗旺斯），希腊和拉丁语的方式——似乎可以——简便地——获得"真相"（或者庞德选择相信），也就是福楼拜"最确切的词"在英语里有时其实无从表达，必须用其他方式。对于庞德而言，翻译是一种方式，去找到神话的真相，历史里的戏剧，政治科学中永恒的悲喜剧。

Inescapably too, all contemporary translators of English are the (bastard) brood of U.S Modernist poet Ezra Pound, who re-modelled English poetry—"made it new"—by ogling enviously the ways in which Chinese, French (Provençal), Greek, and Latin—seemed to be able to get—succinctly—at "Truth" (or so Pound chose to believe), that Flaubert's *le mot juste* was M.I.A. in English on occasion, that one had to find it elsewhere. Translation was a way, for Pound, to locate the Truth in Mythology, the Drama in History, the perpetual Tragicomedy in Political Science ….

In *Mirrors and Windows: East West Poems with Translations*, Anna Yin follows Pound in striving to make contemporary poetry in English accessible to Chinese audiences while, simultaneously, granting English poets a purchase on our contemporary, Chinese peers. Her talent as a translator is a gift of genius to the world. However, it is also necessary diplomacy in an age when global, corporate capitalism calls us to battle stations (again) to make war on each other so as to defend their environmentally destructive and genocidal profiteering. But we poets will have the last word—as always (eventually)—and it is *Peace*.

George Elliott Clarke
4th *Poet Laureate of Toronto (2012-15)*
7th *Parliamentary Poet Laureate of Canada (2016-2017)*

在《镜子与窗户：东西方诗歌翻译》中，安娜追随庞德，力图让中国读者接触当代英语诗歌，同时，赐予英语诗人了解当代中国同行的窗口。她的翻译才华是一种天赋，但是，也是必要的外交，尤其在全球性的，企业化的资本主义呼吁我们（再次）彼此发动战争来保护他们的环境破坏和灭绝种族的暴利的时代。但是我们诗人们将拥有最终的话语权——一如既往（终于获得）——那就是**和平**。

乔治·艾略特·克拉克
第四届多伦多桂冠诗人(2012-15)
第七届加拿大国家桂冠诗人(2016-2017)

It began in an ancient legend that said that one can find truth in mirrors. I discovered my true self in my early thirties when I began writing poetry. Similar things happen to other poets. Poetry not only becomes our windows to see outward but also our mirrors to see inwardly. Later, I was invited to translate poems for some poetry magazines. By helping them, I found translation also serves both as a window and as a mirror. It amazes me that we are all so different, yet also alike. Each poem can lead to another interesting world. And these worlds call us to enter, to explore and to exchange.

During these years I have initiated several cultural exchange projects to promote the poetry of both East and West and to showcase the beauty of both diversity and unity. I gathered various poems from fellow poets and translated them. I also received many requests from poetry editors. So, over the years I have had the honor to translate more than 50 poets' works and most of these translations have been published. With more and more people growing interested in translation and bilingual poetry, I believe it is time to publish my translations as this collection: Mirrors and Windows. I hope this serves as a good resource, and will further stimulate wider and stronger interest and conversation for cross-cultural exchange. I have always felt as Maya Angelou did: "I long, as does every human being, to be at home wherever I find myself." I hope this contribution will open more of these homes.

Anna Yin
Jan 20, 2019

"镜子和窗户"

　　一切始于一个古老的传说：人们在镜子中可以找到真相。三十多岁时我开始写诗，才真正发现真实自我。很多诗人也有类似经历。诗歌不仅是我们向外看的窗户，也成为我们发现内心的镜子。后来，一些诗刊邀请我翻译诗歌。于是我也开始感受到翻译也一样是镜子和窗户。我总是惊叹我们每一个诗人都如此不同，但又如此相似。每首诗都是另一个有趣的世界。这些世界呼唤我们进入，探索和交流。

　　这些年我多次创建文化交流项目，以促进东西方的诗歌，展现多样性和共性的美。我收集诗人的不同诗歌并翻译出来。我也收到诗歌编辑的许多请求。因此我有幸翻译了50多位诗人的作品，大部分翻译作品获得发表。随着越来越多的人对翻译和双语诗歌的兴趣滋长，我相信现在是时候出版这本翻译诗集：镜子和窗户。我希望它成为一个很好的资源，并将进一步激发更广泛和更强烈的对跨文化交流的兴趣和对话。我常常想起玛雅·安吉罗的诗句"像每个人一样，我渴望，当找到自己我就回到了家"。我希望我的努力"镜子和窗户"将构建更多的精神家园。

星子安娜
Jan 20, 2019

PART I

From English to Chinese

From Canada

英诗中译

来自加拿大

What They Prayed For

What they prayed for seemed not much,
and already, despite the dusty weeds
extending to the sky, a possession:
a grassy land, lightly wooded,
rolling, with intricate slopes
and crossed by streams, relieved
by lakes, pools and reedy swamps.
Breezes over the water to suggest
music; and, visible from rises,
the ocean, glinting among the trees,
near so that when you are silent
within yourself it can be heard.
Also shade and shadow:
an openness to the sun,
to the sky, that is yet defended
and moistened by fingers of the earth.
Then a few things will follow
from these first conditions: women
singing in full light and at dusk
before reflecting water;
and some way to live together
that is not a scandal and a shame.

他们祈祷什么

他们所祈祷的似乎并不多，
已有的一份领地，尽管
尘土飞扬的杂草延伸到天空：
一片草地，树木轻微环绕，
起伏着，错综复杂的斜坡
由溪流穿过，再在湖泊，
水域和芦苇沼泽旁静静歇息。
微风吹过，波纹泛漾如音乐；
海洋，在高处可见，从树林丛中
闪闪发光，近得就像当你沉默时
在内心深处可以听得见。
阴处和影子：
那是大地的手指保护着
和润湿的
向着太阳和天空的开放地。
在这些先决条件下，
顺应而来的是：女人
在满堂的光亮中和黄昏的
水镜面前歌唱；
并且以某种方式共同生活
不会成为丑闻和耻辱。

A Narrow Silent Throat

How many nights eaten by rain
have I sat here, dreaming of the world,
this world which is, facing a blank wall,
the sound of ruining water?

Or dreaming by day when the dust
filled the throat and the dry light
burnt all strength from the eyes:
a dream of night with its grateful moisture
out of the sides of the air,
its repose of trees and hedges, its gift
of music in running water?

Dreaming in suffocating nights
of a noon on wooded slopes:
breathable flame, agate that quenches thirst,
and the excellent shape of a maple leaf,
its shadow among a million shadows
conferring a just degree
of darkness upon day: the vegetable
humanizing the light.

Dreaming of a life still possible
in an anguished moment,
a narrow silent throat
where one by one, pulsing and shining,
the unbodied elements pass.

沉默狭窄的喉咙

多少个被雨侵蚀的夜晚
我坐在这里，梦想着这个世界，
面对着一堵空白的墙，
和祸水的声音的世界？

或在白天当尘埃
封满喉咙，干巴巴的光线
焚烧眼里所有力量时，梦想着：
空气流溢湿润的感恩的夜晚，
树木和树篱的安息，以及
流水奏响的音乐礼物？

在窒息的夜晚里我梦想
树木繁茂山坡上的一个中午：
透气的焰体，止渴的玛瑙，
和一片枫叶的优良造型，
它的影子在百万个影子里
授予白天一个刚刚好的暗影：
自然植物赋予阳光人性。

在极度痛苦的时候，我梦想
一种生活仍然可能：
一道沉默狭窄的喉咙那儿
无形的元素一个接一个，
脉动着和闪耀着，
通过。

Poem of Courtly Love

I want to hate what is believed: that darkness
is first and silence best, that the good part
of the word is wind, and the adequate part
an image, that the chance part is the beginning
and the necessary part the end. I want
to sit with you, unable to understand
the book that holds all human story to be
an allegory of our dying
proposals of rebirth. I want this book
we were reading to slip from your lap
as you tremble, seeking courage to surrender,
so the interpretations woven insidiously into plot lines lie face
down in dust, and the story
that starts with your breast
opens in our air — nipples, eyes, tongues
and the words to come
happy in the pause
that is their natural home.

谦雅爱情之诗

我要憎恶那被信奉着的：最初
未知，最好沉默，语言的好处
在于撩来风，意象足够胜任，
由偶然处开始，必要的是目的。我要
和你坐在一起，不去理会
这一本书：它试图诠释
全人类故事是我们不断死而复生
的寓言。我要这本我们曾经读的书
当你颤抖，寻求勇气去屈服时，
从你膝部滑落，
这样这些被阴险地编织成情节线路的解读
只有面朝下地躺在灰尘里，然后故事
就从你的乳房开始，
在我们空中展开——乳头，眼睛，舌头
并且语言不断涌来
在暂停中欣喜
那是它们天然的家园。

Every Step Was into a New World

Every step was into a new world
drenched in memory and longing: these were the dew there.
The sun sparkled in it, the low sun
that pierced the tips of the oak crowns
on the eastern, the far-side banks. A sparkling
that never would leave us, that later we'd know again
in the splendour of a breast shining in lace,
the stirring of birds by the creek,
the fluttering in our struck heart. The sun
shone through the drops of memory,
and the child was wet, chilled
and warmed. The child we were.
He and she purred in nerves and muscles
and brought their eyes close to the places
they could see in the drops, some of the new worlds
of the spot where we'd halted for the morning.

迈入新世界

迈入的每一步都是
记忆和渴望浸透的新世界：这些是那儿的露珠。
太阳在其中闪烁，那低垂的阳光
在东方遥远河岸，
刺穿了橡树冠的顶端。那闪闪的光亮
从不会离弃我们，后来我们
在蕾丝里乳房的荣光里会再次遇见，
在小溪边鸟儿的扑动中，
以及我们怦然心动中遇见。太阳
透过点点滴滴的记忆闪着光，
孩童被润湿了，一个激灵，
又被温暖。我们曾是这孩童呀——
他和她兴奋得嘟嘟嚷嚷
并把眼睛投向那些光亮
以便从点滴记忆里，认出新世界里
我们曾为清晨停伫的那些所在。

Poetry

You chose the right path in life
though as it assures you it abashes you
with crushing beauty — like these lines of Neruda
you desire the way at eleven you desire a girl.
To write just one verse like that. To know
the fruitful softness, the whispering of shadows
in light-sprinkled entrances, the female
strangeness of their male force.
As Neruda's century passed and the astonishment
his coming had aroused decayed, in you it grew.
As the dead fall away, the living is laid bare
more living. You look up from his book
and are in a world more world, and you look up
from that new world and are in his book
more book: another earth, another early home
and childhood. He shelters as he overshadows,
an older brother still a child himself.
You two are orphans, and guarding you through forests
and the eyes of crowds he reaches manhood,
and yet he's still the youth of the good promise,
alpha point of unhewn roads. You feel
abundance and the void rise alert, tender
as they watch him pass and engulf him — a love so dark
you have to long to pierce it repeatedly.

诗

你选择人生正确的路途
虽然它迷醉的美宽慰你
也困惑你——就像你渴望聂鲁达的
诗句如同十一岁时渴望一个女孩。
谱写一首那样的诗。知悉那果实般的柔软，
光线闪烁的入口处的阴影私语，
那男性力量中的女性神秘。
聂鲁达的年代已去，他的来临唤起的惊愕
朽化了，在你这里却生长。
随着死的逝去，活着的被裸露
越发生动。从他的书你仰望，
你抵达一个更普世的世界，
从这个新世界仰望，
你抵达他的更神明的书里：
另一个地球，另一个早期的家园
和童年。一个兄长，自己也不过一个孩子，
他庇护你也让你相形见绌。
两个孤儿的你们，他引导着你穿过森林
和人群的眼睛，抵达成年，
但他仍然是美好承诺的少年，
未凿之路的起始点。
当她们温柔地看着他经过并吞没他，
内心的丰沛和空虚让你警惕——
一种漆黑深切的爱，
你不得不渴望反复地穿戳它。

Advice to the Lovelorn

We are observing Eros,
raddled asteroid, lumpish and erratic,
on a loopy path such that
our planet and that planetoid
just might find themselves
one day trying to inhabit
the same point on their intersecting lines.

So keep a wary eye on it.
It's no sleek bow-directed arrow,
this potato-shaped tumbler
aimed at no particular target in the dark,
just a stranger across a room
that could suddenly become
much too crowded.

Remember this and contemplate
the drowned crater of Chicxulub,
where an asteroid stove in the planet's rib,
turned rock to instant liquid
and instantly back to mountain, a crumpled scab.
And how the noise was heard two thousand miles away —
everyone knew your business. How dark
the skies turned, whole species lying down
to die in the shadows.

给失恋者的忠告

我们正在观察爱神，
破旧的小行星，粗笨古怪，
在周而复始的路上；
我们的地球和它
很可能有一天
在相交线上的同一个点
撞见。

必须警惕它。
它是箭，缺乏好弓平滑引导，
这个马铃薯状的不倒翁
在黑暗中没有特定的目标，
就像只是个陌生人穿过房间
却可能会突然
拥挤不堪。

记住，定神想想
淹没的奇克卢布陨石坑，
那成了地球肋骨里的小行星熔炉，
倒腾着岩石瞬间成熔浆，
再瞬间变回山峦，一个皱巴巴的伤痂。
轰隆声两千英里之外都听得到：
然后，每个人都知道你的悲惨。
天变得多么黑，所有的物种
在阴影中倒下死去。

But remember too —
you can't see that crater now.
The blue gulf washes over it.
Small creatures you'd previously ignored
became more interesting, filled in the gaps.

And always remember,
though nothing will ever be
the same, still you
are bigger than it is.

但是别忘了
现在你看不到那陨石坑。
蓝色波涛在它上面冲刷着。
很多以前你忽略的小动物
变得多么有趣，填补那些隙缝。

永远记住吧，
虽然不可能再象从前了，
你会好好的，没啥大不了。

The Muse of Universes

Once in a trillion years
the muse of universes
claps her hands. And, with that shock
of light, reverses

an aeon of drift, dilution,
the outward-rolling wave
of dark and the illusion
of end times.

A new draft, she orders
and the universe erupts
into rhyme, fields and forces
echoing. She rebuts

formlessness, sparks stanzas
from an alphabet of particles,
spells out what matters, what
radiates, what tickles

the fancy into galaxies
with gravity's feather pen.
She unrolls the scroll of space,
says, There. Now try again.

宇宙缪斯女神

曾经一万亿年前，
宇宙的缪斯女神
拍了一下手。接着，
随着一道闪电，逆转

亿万年的漂移和稀释，
以及向外滚动的黑浪
暗波和末日的
幻象。

新的草案，她责令，
于是宇宙爆发成
韵律，场和力
呼应。她驳斥

无序，从微粒表中
激发诗章，
用引力羽毛笔书写
什么重要，什么闪耀，

什么激励幻想
形成星系。
展开宇宙卷轴，
她说，那儿。现在再试一次。

Jazz Quartet

From the dark solar
mouth, a torrent of cries
breaks: in rainbows.

Soft freight slams the night.
– Wheel-clash. – Pistons
carom thunder over skin.

Plucked throbs arc across
the bridge of the blood, outwalk
all bars.

One hand grabs the ground;
another hammers embers
into stars.

爵士四重奏

从黑管的太阳
口，呐喊如激流
爆发：在彩虹中。

轻骑货车 敲击夜晚。
滚轮轰隆。活塞
碰撞，皮鼓咆哮。

弹拨的颤动 弓弧掠过
血脉之桥 冲出
所有的障碍。

一只手抓住琴阶底部；
另一只锤落余烬
成星。

Ask

Then who can sight the shadows on the wind,
or hear a single note sung by a stone?

Within a calm, feel how the evening light
sighs to diminish. Sense the pain of dawn.

Think the chaotic torment with which clouds
assemble, swell, disperse.
                              Call up the grief
in vanished language, in bulldozed belief.

Ask dying fish what difference: fire and mud.

Tread far enough apart from fear's refrain
to match the pace a forest would have strode
into a meadow, had it not been paved.

Ask through the unlit chambers down your brain.

Ask the last frog, last bird of a species
whether your fouling nest might yet be saved.

问

那么有谁能看到投在风上的阴影，
或者听到石头吟唱的单个音符？

在平静中，感受夜晚的光亮
如何叹息着消逝。觉察黎明之痛。

思考这混乱煎熬与之一起的乌云
聚集，膨胀，驱散。
用已消失的语言和被推平的信念，
              召唤悲伤。

询问垂死的鱼：烈火和淤泥，有什么不同？

踏行足够遥远吧，远离恐惧的重複，
去赶上森林原本可以大步迈入
未铺沥的牧场的步伐。

询问你自己那被黑暗笼罩的脑瓜。

问问濒临灭种的最后一只青蛙，最后一只鸟
你结垢的巢窟是否还可能获救。

Picking Apples

Not Northern Spies,
Nor Granny Smiths. Yours
Plump Russets
Rouged and weighty.
Or whatever.

When I learned to pick apples, two-handed
In the Niagara orchards,
Weighing them in my palms,
The old orchardman showed me.
Letting gravity do its trick.
Lifting them away.

The ripe and wondrous falling.
Their stems curled, a small leaf
Fluttering like a sprouted wing.
Lowering them into the canvas
Cradled on his chest.

And I had no idea then
He was talking about you,
Or about love.

摘苹果

不是"北方间谍",
也不是"姥姥史密斯"。你的
"圆润赤褐"
红艳且有分量。
其实,是什么无所谓。

在尼亚加拉果园里
我学习用双手采摘苹果;
用手掌掂量它们,
老果农给我演示。
撩起再分开,
让自身重力施展魔力。

那成熟和奇妙的下坠。
茎儿卷曲,一小片叶子
像萌芽的翅膀飞舞。
果实低低落到
他围在胸前的布兜里。

当时我并不懂得
他是在说着你,
或者爱情。

Vanishing Cream

for Amy Winehouse

At Wevill's house one desert night
as I lay reading at the window screen,
a moth flew into my lit candle
and fell burning like a torch song.

By the time I snuffed the flame.
wondering if any art was worth
a life — even a dumb insect's —
only the wings' eyes remained.

I watched other moths, less talented,
dance and beat themselves helpless
against the metal mesh, their flutters
the sound of an old film projector

running silent movies, unaccompanied,
the movements of faces overplayed,
each pancaked to reflect a light
shone through them to the future.

My grandmother would remove her face
each night before she went to sleep
with a cream that made her ghostly,
letting the day vanish as if a miracle —

雪花膏

给艾米·怀恩豪斯

在维尔家一个寂寞的夜里
当我置身窗屏旁读书时，
一只飞蛾飞进点着的蜡烛
跌落燃烧着犹如火炬之歌。

等到我掐灭了火焰，
寻思是否有任何艺术值得
付出生命，哪怕是这只暗哑的虫子，
现在只余下翅膀上的眼睛。

我看到其他的飞蛾，天分不足，
飞舞和无助地拍打着翅膀，
撞击着金属网，它们的扑棱声
好似旧式的影片放映机

运转着无声胶片，毫无伴奏，
它们面部的动作被夸大，
每张脂粉脸反射着光
通透着它们向着未来。

我的祖母每晚睡觉前，
会用雪花膏清除面容，
雪花膏让她象鬼似的，
让白天消失得像奇迹：

the same way I thought nature sang
when I woke at dawn to uneasy steps,
my face still pressed against the screen
and a doe's eyes staring back at me.

同工异曲地，清晨我在不安
的脚步声中醒来，脸依然
紧压着窗屏，而一只母鹿
回望我，我以为大自然歌唱。

Imago

My life as larva has ended.

Silken girdle around my middle,
pupa blends with vegetation.

The greening gift of greener cloth,
my chrysalis — the last instar.

A swaddled change that can't be seen.
Internal systems rearranging.

Leather ripe, enclose my bind.
Shrunken leaf, laundry wet.

Pump in air, escape the crippling,
drain of red. *It's time, it's time.*

Dew receives meconium.
Dawn, the quiet. Imago. Up.

成虫

我幼虫阶段的生活已经终结。

丝质腰带缠绕腰部。
虫蛹隐身草木中。

爽绿的衣裳苍翠的礼物，
我的蝴蝶蛹——最后的虫龄期。

襁褓变革不可看见，
内部系统重新排列。

皮囊成熟，围住我圆形饰带。
像皱缩的叶片， 潮湿着洗涤。

鼓进空气，挣脱残跛，
耗尽血色。 *是时候了，是时候了。*

鲜露承接蛹便。
黎明寂静；成虫。挺立。

There Is a Stir, Always

If I hold onto this body the snow will grow inside me
and the winter of my cells will flake
into tiny crystals like six-figured gods,
each arrow tip attempting to make the point of something
as tears flow.

There is a stir, always.

I rise to the cold
to take my place among the fragile stars,
and sleep.

一种涌动，总会在

若我守住这身体，雪便会在我体内生发，
那儿细胞的严冬将会结成
微小的水晶片，好似六像一体的众神，
当泪水流淌时，每支箭锋都
试图指向什么。

一种涌动，总会在。

迎着寒冷，我起身
到脆弱的群星中占取我的位置，
然后，睡去。

Tulips

It is morning
and the tulips I have
never loved well enough
are leaning away from life.
The acacia holds its thorns
on the other side of the window.
See the girl there who
has never felt her breast.
The hard spot is the beginning
of a terror that finds its beauty
in a song we have never heard,
though we sing it well enough.
When the moon comes,
when the night ends, when
there are more seasons than
can be held by rain, lift
with me the cedar bark,
the limbs that lift as spirits.
It is hard now, knowing we
have always known what
the cedar can't forget.
Come along now, leave the tulips,
never sing of her again.

郁金香

清晨
我从来没有好好爱过
的郁金香
低垂着失去生机。
相思树在窗的另一侧
高举着棘刺。
看那儿那个女孩
乳房还青涩着,
硬块却成了恐怖的开始
在一首我们没听过的歌中
搜寻它的美丽,
虽然我们都好好地咏叹。
当月亮出来,
当夜晚结束,
当更多的季节
雨水无法承接,举起
我和雪松树皮,
枝桠向上就象魂灵。
这样的时候好难,就像我们
一直懂得雪松
难以忘怀哪些。
来吧,现在,告别郁金香,
再也不唱起她。

Life

I was the sunshine that cradled your day
that tried to push the clouds away
I was the sand that ran between your toes
when you were four years old
that soon became the rain you danced in
from seven to eleven
And I watched you grow in the glow
of a moon that beamed
when you turned thirteen
How unfair you thought I'd become
when you turned twenty-one
because you lost a few dreams
But I stayed awake when you were out late
I was the stars 'till you turned twenty-eight
And when you found your love
"the one"
I was glimmer in the eye, the blue sky, the sun
Then you turned thirty-one
I became cloud, thunder and shower
there weren't enough minutes to put in your hour
You forgot how to dance in the rain
'till you turned forty all you did was complain
Then you took off your shoes
and went back to the sand
I was now the warmth of your child's hand
At forty-three
you spent more time with me
You began

生活

我是推开云霭
孕育你日子的太阳光彩;
是你四岁时
流串在你脚趾间的沙石,
从你七岁到十一
我很快成为你翩翩起舞的雨季,
我看着你在月光的光亮中
长成了十三年少青葱。
而你到了二十一,
为了失去的几个梦想,
却认为我是不合情理。
但我一直醒着,无论你多晚不归,
我是星辰,相伴你到二十八生辰。
当你找到了你的所爱,
我是眼睛里的闪亮,蓝天和太阳。
然后到了你第三十一个光阴,
我成了乌云,阵雨和雷鸣,
时间总是如此不够,
你忘记如何在雨中漫舞,
四十到了,总是抱怨不停。
后来呢,你脱掉鞋子
回归以往的沙子,
我成为你孩子手心的温暖。
四十三岁你与我一起
度过更多时日并开始理解。
当你迈过五十,
对时常冷淡的我维持暖意。
六十二岁时我们变得亲近

to understand
And when you stood fifty years old
you stayed warm to me even though
at times I was cold
How close we grew
when you turned sixty-two
The breeze was I
that hung your grandchild's kite in the sky
And I'm sorry I made you sad
when I took "the one" away
But I was proud
when you pushed aside that cloud
and cradled me in the sun
for the remainder of our day

我是微风， 在天空中牵引
你孙儿的风筝。 而我很遗憾
带走了那一位， 让你哀伤悲泣；
但我很骄傲，你推开云雾，
安放我们剩下的日子在阳光里。

Self-Composed

It's today
That I can see
Daisies play
At being me.

Beaming gold,
They bend and sway —
Limber, bold,
Anarchic, gay.

Holding out
Their leaves like hands,
They don't shout
Or make demands.

They're quiet,
Quite, but not shy:
Their riot
Is their beauty.

If I seem
A weed to some
Eyes, I dream —
And flower I am.

泰然自得

就在今天
我得以见识
雏菊扮演
原本我自己。

闪着金光，
弯腰轻摇晃：
机敏大方，
自由且舒畅。

捧出绿叶，
像手儿一样
从不索要，
也不去叫嚷。

好生安分，
却并不害羞：
精彩缤纷
朵朵显灵秀。

如某些人
看我似杂草
我梦如真：
花儿，我就是。

Tombeau de Keats

Language fabricates intimates:
The very alphabet pledges incipient pleasantries —
to rollick in letters,
to kiss without kissing ....

(Note the glib efficacy of the tongue
at lying;
or to indulge injurious prophesying;
or, wielding a battering-ram limerick,
to hurl a potentate off a pedestal.)

Keats, I come to you as a back-page spectre,
a wanton haunt,
my unidentifiable shadow
crossing over your lines,
to find in *Thee* —
beyond the grave's beguiling caricature —
arborescent headstone —
Thy iconic Glamour
that cancels the grave's purgatorial visibility.

Thou art never as marginal as a corpse,
but sprout poems like gilded lilies —
opaque ink jetting white sunlight —
la dolce vita of Liberty —
what flowers from your acreage —
as vast as the (Roman) alphabet ....

[Roma (Italia) 15 *février* mmxiv]

济慈墓前

语言编织亲密：
字母表承诺了最初的客套话——
嬉闹在文字里，
不用吻却已经亲吻。

（注意巧舌如簧便于
撒谎，
或放纵灾难性预言，
或者，舞动着重磅打油诗，
将当权者从座位上掀倒。）

济慈，我似尾页的幽灵走向您，
肆意出没，
我无法辨认的魅影
掠过您的诗句，
去发现您——
在坟墓迷惑的讽刺之外——
在树状墓碑之上，
您的图腾魅力
抵消墓地的炼狱模样。

您决不是已逝者而无足轻重，
却是金百合闪亮迸出的诗句——
是晦暗的墨汁喷射的明亮阳光——
是自由的甜蜜生活——
看！您的大地开出的花儿——
和（罗马）字母一样浩瀚。。。

[罗马（意大利）2014年2月15日]

61

Translated from the Spanish

Come, my love, come, this lonely, passionate
Nova Scotian night. Your voice trembles like wings.
Your bones whisper. Under the moon, I stroll
The shadowed road, awaiting your dark eyes
And sandaled feet. My love, if I have to,
I will pace this blue town of white shadows
And black water all night, if I have to.

译自西班牙文

来吧，我的爱，来吧，这寂寞的，充满激情的
新斯科舍的夜晚。你的声音像翅膀一样颤抖着。
你的身骨在低语。月光下，我漫步于
撒满阴影的道路，等待你乌黑的眼眸
和踏着凉鞋的脚步。我的爱，如果必需这样，
我将整晚踱步在这白色阴影
和黑色水域相互交错的蓝色小镇上，如果必需这样。

Exile

for Kwame Dawes

Your scuttled *pays* floats — fiery — in the ether;
Blazing, it vomits smudge-smoke. Your mind chars
Black because you yaw — moth-like — too near flames.
You douse your dream-scorched brain with slave-sweat rum —
The only gold you can own, corroding
Your liver. Your anthem plays to gunfire.
  When you think about it (when you can breathe) —
After all the lies that frame nostalgia,
All the dead faces that occupy photographs,
All the slain lovers pitched into ditches,
Your eyes itch and ache with water, then dry —
Curling like dead leaves, starving for gold fire.

流亡

致夸梅·道斯

你破碎的国家漂浮在火热的苍穹中；
灼热的，它呕吐污秽的烟雾。你的头脑烧成
黑色，因为你——像飞蛾一样——偏离航向，趋近火焰。
你用汗水拼来的浓酒（这唯一你可拥有的金子，
正腐蚀着你的肝脏）去浸泡你被梦想烧焦的大脑。
此刻你的国歌在枪声中奏响。
当你想到它（当你可以呼吸）：
所有的那些编织乡愁的谎言，
所有的那些充斥照片的死尸面容，
所有的被诛的爱人投进沟渠之后，
你的眼睛又痒又痛满是泪水，然后干枯
像卷曲的枯叶，渴望着熊熊烈焰。

Ode to Machiavelli

I.
That dry-bone, hard-ass intellectual knows that
if —
the very word —
inaugurates godly *Magic*, devilish *Power*.

If destroys *Innocence*.
It's the first word the Serpent addressed to Eve.

II.
He looks out upon Venice:
The water is like moving glass:
No wretched foaming here
as on the British monarch's shores,
that urine-scoured waste.

He drafts the Bible's rival canticle —
an unrivalled canticle —
los canticos intellectual.
To read him is to drink in *Power*;
more intoxicating than *Venery*.

III.
If one reads Machiavelli, one learns:

The beauty of *History* is struggle;
the history of *Beauty* is struggle;
the struggle of *History* is beauty;

马基雅维利颂歌

I
那冷酷，强硬的智者知道
假如——
这个非同寻常的字
创建神似的戏法，魔状的权力。

假如摧毁纯真。
它是蛇对夏娃说的第一个字。

II
他往威尼斯望去：
流水平静如移动的玻璃：
这里没有恼人的泡沫
如那英国女王的海岸上
象尿液冲刷着的废物。

他起草了圣经的敌对颂歌——
无与伦比的颂歌——
知性的圣歌。
品读他就好比在权力中畅饮；
比性交更醉人。

III。
如果一个人阅读马基雅维里，他会学到：

历史的美在于斗争；
美的历史在于斗争；
历史的斗争是美；

the history of *Struggle* is beauty;
the beauty of *Struggle* makes history.

But the struggle for *Beauty* is never "history."

[Ottawa (Ontario) 23 *mai* mmxii]

斗争的历史是美；
斗争的美创造历史。

但是争取美永远不会成为"历史"。

[渥太华（安大略省）5月23日2012]

Experience 1: 1-9

History is nothing like what is reported.
(Hard to drain light from mud.)

Trumpets don't usher in Heaven.

Truth blinds, but Deceit dazzles.

Flames that don't gleam are smoke.

Manure gerrymanders gardens:
Eden flowers from shit.

Fine wine refines urine.

Politics is PREJUDICE.

Behind these black letters?
White bone, invisible breath.

Bread is eternal.
But your words?

[Zurich, Switzerland. 14 September, 2011]

经验1：1-9

历史从来不是报道所述。
（泥巴哪能透出光？）

天堂里无需号角迎宾。

真理盲目，**骗局**却眩目。

不闪耀的火焰只是烟雾。

败类操纵花园：
伊甸园花自粪中来。

美酒醇化尿液。

政治就是**偏见**。

这些黑色的文字背后是什么？
是白色的骨头，是隐没的喘息。

面包是永恒的。
但是你的言语呢？

[瑞士苏黎世。 2011年9月14日]

When He Died, He Took One Last Poem with Him

for Earle Birney

He lived his life like a leaf
dancing and singing
from a hazel bough
in winter, he'd simply move
the tree indoors

His words etched
a million faces on paper
burned a memory in metaphor
cities of parchment
exploded like firecrackers

His hands molded pictures
like a sculptor he'd fashion
shadows in holes
and everyone would gasp
at their exactness

The ritual was a myth

He sleeps with one last poem
as a blanket to cover
the decay of genius
now and forever

I.B. 伊斯科夫

他死时，带走最后一首诗

致厄尔伯尼

像一片来自榛树
的叶子飞舞歌唱
他活着
冬季来临，安详地
把树移居室内

他的诗句在纸上
蚀刻了百万张脸
在隐喻中烧灼了记忆
羊皮纸的城市
鞭炮一样爆破

如雕塑家一样
他的手塑造了形像
塑造洞中的阴影
每个人都惊叹
他的准确无误

仪式成为了一个神话

他睡着伴着最后一首诗
就像毯子覆盖
天才的衰败
现在和永远

Ulysses

The universe is made of stories,
not of atoms.
        — Muriel Rukeyser

When Ulysses grew frail he lived in Parsons,
on the second floor of a rest home.
On all sides Monongahela National Forest
swept over ridge after ridge of West Virginia.
Blackgum, stave oak, sourwood
flamed up in mixed stands:
a searing red and orange as the frost
came heavy to the hill country.

King of Ithaca, mighty warrior
of Trojan battles, how then is this sick,
old man Ulysses? Ah, grandfather,
your depleted bones and black lungs
have betrayed you into the hands
of nurses, of doctors too young, perhaps,
to understand a miner's pride.

But in your green season, you rose in the dark
to light fire where fire had died,
calling flames from roses of death
to warm the home, heat water for washing.
A wife and eight children up near Chestnut Ridge.

詹姆斯·迪尔

尤利西斯

> *宇宙是由故事，*
> *而非原子构成的。*
> ——穆里尔·鲁凯泽

当尤利西斯变得虚弱时，他住在
帕森斯，休养所的二楼。
四面都是一座座被莫农加希拉
国家森林席卷的西弗吉尼亚的山脊。
黑胶，酸模和橡树一棵棵
苒苒地错杂着挺立：
在浓烈秋霜降临这个山区时，
成为一片灼热的火红和橙色。

伊萨卡国王，特洛伊战役中
的伟大战士，怎么就这么病歪病歪，
老迈的尤利西斯？啊，爷爷
您枯竭的骨骼和黑烂的肺脏
背叛了您，转向护士和医生之手，
只是她们太年轻，哪能
理解一个矿工的荣耀。

那是在青春年华，黑暗中您站起来
为栗树岭的妻子和八个孩子，
在火已熄灭处点燃炉火，
从死神玫瑰中唤取火焰
给家里送暖，供热水洗涤。

Then out into autumn paths emblazoned
by scarlet hands of sourwood, burning lobes
of blackgum, from every tree a song of birds
heading south . . .

Finally, to end alone in Parsons wondering
whose lungs you can use to breathe,
whose throat to sing.

然后进入秋季的小径那儿被酸木的
猩红手掌，和黑胶燃烧的叶片饰染，
那儿每棵树上传来
往南迁徙的鸟鸣。。。

最后呢，您孤独一人在帕森斯，
思量着谁的肺腑您可以借用，
谁的喉咙去鸣唱。

Poem

a poem should be a microscopic watch
worn by an invisible hand
belonging to a several-handed midget
in the somber clothes of a blackbird
hiding in the gold-frosted corn field
by a serpentine road near a quaint pond
where imaginary blue bullfrogs rhapsodize
the Sunday blues of their ancestors
who lived by that time schedule
of the microscopic watch worn by an invisible
mouse trainer who had a terrible phobia
for mixed metaphors & white cats
with silver blue eyes of the Orient

诗

一首诗应该是一只微观手表
被一个看不见的手佩戴
来自那穿着黑鹂的阴沉衣服
的有着几只手的侏儒
隐藏在古怪池塘的蜿蜒路旁
的金灿灿的玉米田
那儿假想的蓝色牛蛙们高歌
他们祖先的周日蓝调
祖先遵从着那只微观手表
的时间表，而手表被隐身的
老鼠教练戴着，他患有可怕的恐惧症：
害怕混淆的隐喻和
有着东方的银蓝色眼睛的白猫。

Being Human

I am reading Rumi
reading Tu Fu
and thinking of being human
last summer
Marty and I
slept in the farmhouse loft
under French heaven near Vitteaux
and we lay in our separate cots
like boys at camp
laughing, talking silly
making fun of everyone
we were mostly ourselves, middle aged men
with the window open
to starlight
and the evening breath of the fields

look up at the slant of ceiling
the slant of beams
this room was built
for dreaming
and we were giddy as lads
with happy lives, not
old Tu Fu, his sadness settled
like shadows, like rivers
like cold stones of winter
and the bitter darkness of long nights
and the lonesome insomnia
of small hours

做人

读着鲁米，
读着杜甫，思潮起伏。
去年夏天，
马蒂和我
睡在农家阁楼，
在阿尔奈苏维托附近的法国天堂下，
象野宿的男孩
我们躺在各自的行军床上，
傻笑，瞎说，
拿每个人取乐。
两个中年男人自由自在，
窗户敞开着
通向星光，田野的清新空气弥漫。

仰望斜斜的天花顶，
斜斜的木梁，
这个房间象为梦境而设，
而我们是那不谙世的少年，
乐颠颠的。
不象老杜，
他的悲伤潜伏如阴影，
如河流，如寒冬冰冷的岩石，
那失眠孤寂的时时刻刻
和漫长而苦涩的黑夜，
像生与死神秘的美丽
和灵魂里不可解脱的愤怒。
我们的心
拒绝沉默，

like the mystical beauty of death and dying
and the inescapable anger of the soul
our hearts refusing the silence
with a lovely slowing exhalation
as we each become
more pensive in
the loosening limbs of slumber
relaxing our hands like unfurled leaves
and pressing our faces to linen

meanwhile great rivers of the earth
the Tigris and Euphrates
the Yangtze
the Amazon of my father's last days
flow on
and what would I buy
from the famous floating markets of Bangkok
I would purchase the rains of remember
I would purchase the stars of recall
and what to preserve in a poem
but the drenching of darkness with light.

当呼吸渐渐舒缓，
身体松驰在睡眠中，
手象叶子舒展，脸紧贴着床单，
我们进入冥思。

与此同时，
大地宏伟的河流啊，
底格里斯河、幼发拉底河
扬子江，
亚马逊河随着我们祖先们最后的日子
流逝着
在曼谷的水上市场
我能买到什么
我愿购买如雨的记忆，
我愿购买如星的回想，
而诗歌能保留什么，
那些湿透的黑暗中的光亮。

Silver Bridge

You remember seeing the Danforth bridge —
strung with threads —
an angel harp with you inside it
like an astounded moth
in a spider's web,
or a bead in a dream catcher.

You travel inside this threaded instrument
on your way to violin lessons
like you might be Jonah
inspecting the whale's intercostals,
or Noah's offspring
revisiting the ribs of the arc.

You ponder the workmanship
of this half-mile of elaborate lines,
taut on the frets of the bridge,
and recall a Buddhist poem
about a musician who spent his life
stringing and un-stringing his lute,

but never played.

And you realize that this weave of silver filaments,
this enticing spun silk
glinting in the September sunlight

银桥

你记得看见丹福思桥——
被银线牵引着——
一个天使竖琴将你围住
像一只在蜘蛛网里
被震惊的飞蛾，
或一粒珠子在梦的捕获者手里。

你在这丝线密绕的乐器里穿行
去往你的小提琴课路上
好像你会如约拿
检查鲸鱼的肋骨间隙，
或挪亚的后代
重新掂量方舟的梁骨。

你凝思这半英里
精密丝线的工艺，
紧绷桥梁的烦恼，
想起一首佛教徒诗
关于一个音乐家度过了一生
为他的琵琶续弦解弦，

却从来没有弹过。

你意识到这银色的锦绣编织，
这样诱人的绢丝
在九月阳光下闪闪发光

Is a trap, a cage, a publicly-funded skein
to prevent you
from leaping to your death.

是一个陷阱，一只牢笼，一袭因公资助的绞纱
　为了防止你
　　跃向死亡。

Dragon Fruit

You are sitting at a round table
with eleven other guests, slicing gently
into avocado and lime.
There is wine.
Some of you have broken bread.

Music wafts from the outer room, mingled
with smells of roasting yam and maple sugar.

You choose the rustic olive loaf,
tear off a crust, lick your fingers,
their rosemary salt.

On each plate, a slice of something milky-clear.
Dots like poppy seeds or inner kiwi specks.
It must be fruit, but it could be other, almost
of the sea, sushi-like anemone.

Will it be saline or sweet?

A wet drip sticks to your fingertip.
Touch it to your tongue:
sweet water, heavy, a little scent
of something from your Grandma's rose kitchen.

You are told this is Chinese Dragon Fruit, are shown
the green scales with red tips
on the tuberous shape, recalling
a childhood puppet, amaryllis bulb,
the komodo dragon's poison claws,

火龙果

你和十一位客人
坐在圆桌旁，轻轻地
把油梨和酸橙切成薄片。
红酒备好了。
有人掰碎了面包。

音乐从外屋飘来，混杂着
烤红薯和枫糖的味道。

你挑了乡土的橄榄面包，
撕下一片面包皮，舔了舔手指，
迷迭香盐滋味。

每个碟子上放着一片乳状透明物。
小圆点像罂粟籽或奇异果籽。
一定是水果，也有可能是别的，大概
来自海里，寿司状的海葵。

会咸吗，还是甜的呢？

湿湿的一滴粘在你指尖。
用舌头触及：
甜的，浓烈，些许香味
仿佛来自祖母的玫瑰厨房。

你被告知这是中国火龙果，
那管状上绿色的鳞片连着
红色的尖梢，让你想起了
童年的木偶，孤挺花鳞茎，
科莫多巨蜥的毒爪。

a little choke of fear in your throat.

Look at the others'
curiosity around the circle—
some slurp it up in sections,
some decline. You imagine
yellow rays of Asian splendor like the sun
penetrating this delicacy.

Possible only in this era.
Eating fruit out of season—
you can ingest a patch of light
from another corner of the world.

你倒吸一口凉气。

看着别人
好奇地围成一圈——
有人分节吸取。
有人谢绝。你想象
亚洲火龙的黄色光芒，太阳一般
穿透这美味。

品尝不合时宜的水果
只有在当代才有可能——
你可以摄取一片光亮
从世界的另一个角落。

Guanyin Lamp

A Guanyin lamp left burning in a closed storefront.
Light without mercy on your small right-hand finger,
On your head and broken finger.

Here's the boy, the girl, faces stroked by your robe.
You're a hollow never filled
And your face is serene.

The "Cries of the World" unheard behind plate glass.
Dust-streaked kitsch, you dream of sound.
I dream of our rescue.

All that's empty was once filled past the brim.
The fountains unstoppable —
Air, blood, song.

If I could rub your cheek, place a finger on your brow,
Find scrolled below the lotus the poems of — or — ,
Not a worker's lament.

One of the numbered innumerable, faces lowered.
Compassion cast in clay.
The moon in tears.

Blanched pomegranate at your feet. Fish mid-leap.
Shipped by freighter, globe-poised Guanyin, unhearing …
Unbury me.

观音灯

在一个打烊的店面，一盏观音灯燃烧着。
在你的小右手指，头顶和残破的手指上，
光亮不带怜悯。

男孩，女孩，脸孔被你长袍抚摸。
你，永远充不满的空心，
脸上一片安详。

"世上的叫喊"在平板玻璃后被屏蔽。
粉尘媚俗，你梦想声音。
我梦想我们的得救。

曾经满溢的一切现在空空。
不停息的喷泉：
空气，血液，哭声。

如果我能擦拭你的脸颊，安放手指在你的额前，
寻找卷在荷花下面的诗篇，亦或，
不是一个工匠的哀叹。

无数中的一个，面孔朝下。
粘土中恻隐之心。
月亮流着泪水。

你脚下石榴失色。海鱼飞跃。
由货轮运达，处世不惊的观音，还是不闻不问。。。
把我挖出这死寂的坟墓吧。

Walk me through the flames. We'll emerge soft and fearless
With a thousand arms each
And a mouth for every wound.

We'll perch on chemical clouds, rolling dragon dust.
Pain glazed from our lips.
The planet run to extremes.

An engine misfires. I rest my forehead on glass.
Moth-hearted, lost in adulthood,
Thirsty for light.

All the cries of the world! Something to sell, swallow, sorrow.
Your uncontrolled kindness
Rains on the void.

伴我走过火焰。让我们刚柔并济
每个有着一千只臂膀，
每道创伤都会开口倾诉。

我们将栖息在冶炼云上，搅动龙尘。
自我们嘴唇彩釉疼痛。
我们的行星转向极致。

可发动机失着火。前额贴在玻璃上休憩的我，
心像飞蛾，在成年后迷失，
饥渴着光亮。

世上所有的叫喊！总有东西在出售，吞咽，哀泣。
而你那疏于操控的善意，
像雨点，一点，一点
落在虚空上。

The Chinese Man

In the afternoon
the old Chinese man
kneels in a garden.

The sunlight flickers—
a golden tapestry on the red wall.

Jazz from an old film echoes;
a broken leaf falls.

He feels for a single nail,
sets it on the wood,
hammers straight as thought.

Resolute he is,
the golden tapestry on the red wall.

中国男子

午后
一位中国老人
跪在花园里。

阳光闪烁，
金色挂毯在红墙上。

老影片里的爵士乐回想;
一片碎叶落下。

他触摸到一颗钉子，
安置它在木头上，
像预期的那样锤直.

他坚决果断，
金色挂毯在红色的墙壁上。

Winter

So this is winter —
And what remains of the world

Now that autumn has left us,
Gone underground with the

Once luminous grasses and the husks
And seeds of all the left-behinds.

This is the cold season.
Learn to endure it.

Winter teaches us to love the long
Liturgies of ice, the sudden stopping of water

Before the black flock of birds
Lift blindly off the pond.

冬季

那么这就是冬季——
又有什么残存于世

既然秋季离开了我们,
去到地下

和曾经茂盛的草,果壳,
以及所有剩余的种子。

这是冰冷的季节。
学会去忍受它。

冬季教我们去爱冗长
祷文式的冰,这突然截住的水

在一群黑鸟盲目地
自池塘升起以前。

Angel Guardian

He's lazy and never around
when I need him
I drive down
to the coffee shop
in the early morning
and find him reading the paper
or talking to the locals
I want to tell him
he's not taking this seriously
— he's supposed to watch over me
He shrugs and says the rules
have changed
I can reach him on Facebook
Besides he carries a cell phone
I want to ask how he got this job
Why me? Why him?
Luck of the draw, he shrugs
our birthdays the same
we both have bad eyes
a hearing problem
and can't eat spicy foods
But where was he in October 1950
the afternoon on Wyandotte
when I was four
and I ran between
two parked cars?
He was there, he says
coming out of the pool hall

守护天使

他懒散，当我需要时
从不在附近
早晨我开车
到咖啡店
发现他在读报
或者与当地人聊天
我想告诉他
他没有认真对待
——他应该照看我
他耸耸肩，说规则
已改变
我可以在脸书上找到他
他也随身携带一部手机
我想问他是怎么得到这工作的
为什么是我？为什么是他？
抽到的运气呗，他耸耸肩
我们的生日在同一天
我们眼睛都不好
还有听力问题
不能吃辛辣的东西
但是，1950年10月
在怀恩多特的那个下午他在哪？
我才四岁
跑在两辆车之间。
他在那里，他说，
走出台球厅
来救我
在暖热的地面上

to save me
to cup my bleeding head
on the warm pavement
to glare at the driver
who stood in the open door
of his Ford worried sick
that I might die
He was there, he said
otherwise I might not
be having this conversation
and he was there again
when I lay curled up
and unconscious
in the hospital room one winter
swearing at the hospital staff
after bowel surgery
and he touched my lips
with his index and middle fingers
and quieted me
Besides, he's always there
and there's no point
having this conversation
— he's so far ahead
and knows so much more:
a hundred different languages
names of every star
in the universe, the physics
of flying, and the winner
of the Stanley Cup
every year till the
end of time

抱我流血的头
眼睛瞪向
那站在车门开着的
福特车旁
担心我可能会死的司機
他在那里，他说，
否则我们不可能会
有这次谈话
他再次在那里
当一个冬天
我蜷缩着
昏迷在医院的病房里
在肠道手术后
咒骂医院的工作人员
他用他食指和中指
碰触我的嘴唇
让我安静下来
此外，他总是在那里
——这样谈话真没意义
他是如此遥遥领先
并知道这么多：
上百种不同的语言
宇宙中每颗星的名字
飞行物理学，以及每年斯坦利
冠军杯的获胜者
直到生命的尽头

Nonsense Poem, or I Like

I like the fact that the light just turned green,
and I like the expression "creamin' in her jeans."

I like the seagull who just shit on my head,
and I like the mongrel who's only playing dead.

I like the secretary who says vanilla, not manila,
and I like the paperweight shaped like a gorilla.

I like the coarseness, the smell of a horse's mane,
I like the careerist who desires a little fame.

I like living, but I don't like feeling lost, and I like
the daffodils — insistent, resilient in the frost.

废话诗，又名我的嗜好

我嗜好光线刚刚变绿的事实，
我嗜好牛仔裤的"爆操"字样。

我嗜好刚在我头上拉屎的海鸥，
而且嗜好只是假扮死人的杂种。

我嗜好说香草不说马尼拉的秘书
我嗜好样子像大猩猩一样的纸镇。

我嗜好马鬃毛的粗糙和气味，
我嗜好渴望混出名气的野心家。

我嗜好生活，但我不嗜好迷失，我嗜好
水仙花——坚定执着，风霜中顽强挺立。

I've Tasted My Blood

If this brain's over-tempered
Consider that the fire was want
And the hammers were fists.
I've tasted my blood too much
To love what I was born to.

But my mother's look
Was a field of brown oats, soft-bearded;
Her voice rain and air rich with lilacs:
And I loved her too much to like
How she dragged her days like a sled over gravel.

Playmates? I remember where their skulls roll!
One died hungry, gnawing grey porch-planks;
One fell, and landed so hard he splashed;
And many and many
Come up atom by atom
In the worm-casts of Europe.

My deep prayer a curse.
My deep prayer the promise that this won't be.
My deep prayer my cunning,
My love, my anger,
And often even my forgiveness
That this won't be and be.
I've tasted my blood too much
To abide what I was born to.

我尝过自己的鲜血

如果这个头颅淬火过头，
请考虑火是必须的，
而锤头就是拳头。
我尝过太多自己的鲜血，
无法喜欢我出生注定。

但我母亲的面容
是一片棕色燕麦地，带着柔软的细须；
她的声音像弥漫丁香的细雨和空气：
我如此深爱她，因此讨厌
她像拖拽雪橇在石渣路上度日。

伙伴吗？我记得他们的头骨在哪里滚动！
一个死于饥饿，啮咬着灰色门廊的板条；
一个跌落，着地时血肉飞溅；
还有许多的许多
分解成一个个原子
在满是蠕虫的欧洲荒野。

我深切的祷告是一个诅咒。
我深切的祷告是这一切将不再的承诺。
我深切的祷告是我的技俩，
我的爱、我的愤怒
甚至往往是我的宽恕
这些都不要一而再。
我尝过太多自己的鲜血，
无法忍受我出生注定。

Couple Sharing a Peach

It's not the first time
we've bitten into a peach.
But now at the same time
it splits — half for each.
Our "then" is inside its "now,"
its halved pit unfleshed —

what was refreshed.
Two happinesses unfold
from one joy, folioed.
In a hotel room
our moment lies
with its ode inside,
a red tinge,
with a hinge.

情侣共享一颗桃

这不是第一次了
我俩共咬一颗桃。
但如今同一时刻
它裂开：均分正好。
果核半开着裸露，
今朝携往事缠绵，

旧情刷新再复燃。
两份幸福自一份喜乐，
扩展再对折。
客栈内，
良宵时分
续情缘——
亦如蜜桃果核，
亦如并蒂情歌。

Why I am Not a Buddhist

I love desire, the state of want and thought
of how to get; building a kingdom in a soul
requires desire. I love the things I've sought —
you in your beltless bathrobe, tongues of cash that loll
from my billfold — and love what I want: clothes,
houses, redemption. Can a new mauve suit
equal God? Oh no, desire is ranked. To lose
a loved pen is not like losing faith. Acute
desire for nut gateau is driven out by death,
but the cake on its plate has meaning,
even when love is endangered and nothing matters.
For my mother, health; for my sister, bereft,
wholeness. But why is desire suffering?
Because want leaves a world in tatters?
How else but in tatters should a world be?
A columned porch set high above a lake.
Here, take my money. A loved face in agony,
the spirit gone. Here, use my rags of love.

为什么我不是佛教徒

我爱欲望，那种想要的感觉以及痴迷
如何去获取；在灵魂里建立王国之境
需要欲望。我爱孜孜以求的所得所觅：
你，裹在无束腰浴袍里，卷舌的现金
闲置我皮夹里 – 我也爱想要的：锦衣，
房子，赎买。一套新潮的浅紫套装
能等同上帝吗？哦，不，欲望排着名次。
失去心爱的笔不等同失去信仰。对奶油
果仁蛋糕的迫切渴望被死神驱走，
但盘子上的蛋糕有着它的意义，
即使爱情危在旦夕，一切已不紧要。
我为母亲要健康；我为妹妹，曾经沧桑，
要完好。只是为什么欲望会煎熬？
因为欲望使得世界支离破碎吗？
世界还要应该怎样，除了支离破碎？
一座圆柱门廊高高矗立在湖泊之上。
来，拿去我的钞票。心爱的脸在痛苦中，
精神殆尽。来，用上我褴褛破旧的爱。

The Flaw

The best thing about a hand-made pattern
is the flaw.
Sooner or later in a hand-loomed rug,
among the squares and flattened triangles,
a little red nub might soar above a blue field,
or a purple cross might sneak in between
the neat ochre teeth of the border.
The flaw we live by, the wrong color floss,
now wreathes among the uniform strands
and, because it does not match,
makes a red bird fly,
turning blue field into sky.
It is almost, after long silence, a word
spoken aloud, a hand saying through the flaw,
I'm alive, discovered by your eye.

瑕疵

手工制作模式最美妙的事情
在于瑕疵。
或迟或早，在手织地毯中，
正方形和扁平的三角形之间，
一小点红心可能飙升在蓝色领域之上，
或紫色十字会悄悄嵌入
整齐的齿赭边界。
我们将就着的瑕疵，错色的丝线
如今盘绕在清一色棉缕中，
并且，因为它不相称，
让一只红色的小鸟飞翔
把蓝色当成天空了。
这就好像，经过长时间的沉默，一句话
大声说出，一只手透过瑕疵在说，
啊，*鲜活的我*，被你发现啦。

Single Traveler

What is this love that is my life's companion?
Shape-changer, sometimes faceless, this companion.

Single traveler, I wander a wasting world
awaiting the much anticipated Companion.

A trillium covered wood one April day
served as a nearly consummate companion.

A horse, two dogs, some cats, a blue macaw
each in its turn became a loyal companion.

Behind the loved embrace, a face of light-
demon or angel-lures me from my companion.

The street of love is neither wide nor narrow.
Its width depends on me and my companion.

Am I too bound and blinded by coarse wrappings
ever to know true love as my companion?

O Poet, squanderer of time and talents
why do you search for love as your Companion?

孤旅者

这爱是什么样才是我一生的伴侣？
变形者，时时不露面的，这个伴侣。

孤旅者，我徜徉一个荒废的世界
等待着这个期盼向往良久的伴侣。

四月天一块被三叶草覆盖的木头
担任了我的似乎完美精湛的伴侣。

一匹马两条狗几只猫和蓝色鹦鹉，
每一个轮流成为一个忠诚的伴侣。

在爱的拥抱的背后，光亮的面孔——
魔鬼或天使——诱惑我离开我的伴侣。

爱情的街道既不宽阔也不狭窄。
它的宽度取决于我和我的伴侣。

是我太约束或蒙蔽于粗糙的包装
以致于不懂真爱才是我的伴侣？

哦，诗人，岁月和才华的浪子
为何要找寻爱成为你的伴侣？

Exit Poll

Advice to the New Leader

1. Promises are made to be broken,
              — like rotten eggs —
    but not until the morning
                        after the election.

2. The current state of affairs
            is merely your reaction
    to mistakes *others* made in the past.

3. Give the people what they want
    — visions of fresh young faces,
      sunny summer picnics, and
      reduced deficit spending —
    but don't let them realize
        a better tomorrow.

4. Because the next administration
                will have to
            take it
        back!

5. Fiscal restraint is what makes
                our civilization *great* —
        or, at least, it will keep
            the current system
    chugging along a bit longer.

帕特里克·康纳斯

票站调查

——致新领导的建议书

1.许下的承诺就是用来打破，
　　——像烂鸡蛋一样——
　　不过要等到
　　　　　　　选举后的那个早上。

2.目前的状况
　　只是你应对别人
　　过往错误的反应。

3.给人们他们想要的
　　——年轻鲜活面孔的愿景，
　　　　阳光灿烂的夏日野餐，和
　　　　减少的赤字支出——
　　但不要让他们明白
　　　　一个更好的明天。

4.因为下届政府
　　　　将不得不
　　　收
　　回！

5.财政约束，好呀
　　　　它使我们文明伟大——
　　至少，它将维系
　　　　当前系统
　　挣扎延续更长久一些。

6. A balanced budget
          should *almost* make up
     for all those pesky poor people.

6.预算平衡吗

应该差不多弥补

所有烦人的穷人。

Spirit Tree

I introduced myself to the tree
in Prospect Cemetery.
"Hi, Tree," I said.
"Nice weather we're having."
Prospect Cemetery is a place I like to walk
But I never really notice the trees.
The tombstones kind of steal the show.
That and the stuffed bears and colourful
pinwheels and mountains of cheap
fabric carnations and creepy
black-and-white photographs everywhere.
Nevertheless, there are also lots of trees
in Prospect Cemetery. Maybe a ratio
of 10 to 1, tombstones to trees.
That's a lot of fertile soil, if you ask me,
for the dead to rest in. Or maybe
that's a lot of dead for the trees to feed on.
Ecology was never my forte. That's
kind of why I'm here I suppose
talking to this tall tree of a variety
I am not knowledgeable enough
to name. I've read somewhere it
might be useful, healing in fact,
to talk to trees, better yet, to pick
a tree that might indeed be your
special tree of life, your spirit tree.
I picked this tree because it's tall
and its leaves form triangular shelves

灵树

在展望公墓
我對著树介绍自己
"嗨，树，"我说
"今天天气真好"
展望公墓是我喜欢散步的地方
但我从没真正注意到这些树。
那些墓碑抢去了风头。
墓碑和毛绒熊，彩色的
纸风车以及成堆的廉价
人造康乃馨和随处可见
瘆人的黑白照片。
尽管如此，展望公墓里
还是树木良多。也许
墓碑和树是10比1。
如果你问我，这可是沃土，
让死者安息。或者也许
对树木来说，足够多的养料。
生态学从来不是我的强项。这也是
我想要和这颗高大树木交流
却连树名都叫不上的原因。
在某处我读到和树木交谈
可能有用，确切说，治疗作用，
尤其是选择一棵树，兴许真就是
你命中之树，你的灵树。
我选了这棵树，因为它很高
并且叶子形成三角形的架子
就像我设想的天梯
蜿蜒着伸上苍穹。

much like my idea of staircases
winding up into the sky.
"Sorry, Tree, I didn't catch that."
I guess I should be paying attention
now that I started this conversation.
I'm just not really trained in this
type of green dating and I feel sort
of embarrassed, not just by the act
of soliciting a tree in the middle
of the day in a respectable graveyard
but also by the very real and fierce
desire I have to be loved by this tree
in return. "I'm sorry, Tree, I didn't
catch that." I don't speak Tree well.
That's for sure. Maybe I should draw
a picture. "Would you like that, Tree?"
Maybe we should stop all this pretense,
and I should do what I came here to do
and drop to my knees.

"对不起，树，我没听清楚。"
我想既然是我先开口的，
我应该留心。
只是我没有受过这种绿色约会
的训练，同时还有点尴尬，
不单是因为大白天的在一个庄严的
墓地里征询一棵树，
也是因为我非常真切而强烈的
愿望：作为回报这些树必须爱我。
"对不起，树，我不懂。"
毫无疑问。我不知如何
好好和树说话。也许我应该
画画。"你想要吗，树？"
也许我们应该停止所有这些伪装，
我应该做我来这里该做的事：
跪求在地。

Window

A window gathered light from the sky
and argued for life in a bad time,
as amid gesticulating boughs
of a stripped maple, its crooked fingers
raise in bitter emphasis,
an unseen orator spoke in mime.
The wind exhaled October like a threat
and stirred the leaves to riot
that merely loitered in their discontent.
The house itself leaked spirit
through the roof and walls,
received the cold airs passively,
those deputations bearing
seasonal warrants of arrest,
but the heart,
not ready to renounce its true estate,
saw the sky framed like a constitution
where the window gathered light.

窗户

窗户聚集来自天空的光亮
在糟糕时刻为生活辩护
就像在一棵树皮剥落的
枫的指手画脚枝桠间，用弯曲的手指
夸张酸苦地举起，
一个隐形的演说家无声的演讲。
十月的风宛如一种胁迫
搅拌着树叶骚动
但仍然滞留在它们的牢骚中。
透过屋顶和墙壁
房子泄露自身的精神气儿，
只得接纳寒冷气流，
如同法定代理者带着
季节的逮捕令，
但是心，
不准备放弃其真正的领地，
看见在窗户聚集的光亮处
天空被架构成一道宪法。

The Season

I remember him, whoever he was,
after work on the twenty-fourth, his tie
straight, the knot holding through a day,
I supposed, of hands shaken, calls returned,
files clewed up, satisfaction given and got.
I was pushing a cart of all that new marriage
might need to eat: potatoes, carrots,
and a turnip, bread and milk and eggs.
Among the meats I watched him, admired
the overcoat that cost him a bundle
at Tip Top, the London, or The Model Shop.
Guessed him thirty-five and unspoused.
At the cooler, he lifted two Cornish hens,
eyed them through plastic wrap, weighed them, and chose,
then he walked up some aisle of memory
to pass in and out of sight at year's end
among carols, angels, and guiding stars.

圣诞

我记得他，不管他姓甚名谁，
二十四日完工后，他的领带
笔直，领结保持完好一整天，
我设想，他定满足赠与和收获
在握手，回电和文档收卷中。
而我推着一车新婚的所有的
可能需要吃的：土豆，胡萝卜，
青萝卜，面包圈，牛奶和鸡蛋。
在肉类摊之间，我注视他，憧憬
他的外衣出品自顶呱呱，伦敦
或模特店，不定耗费多少银子。
我猜他大概三十五岁，还没配偶。
他拿起冷柜的两只科尼什母鸡，
透过塑料包装观察，衡量，再选择，
然后他走过记忆的某个过道，
走进又走出迷茫模糊的视线
在年底颂歌，天使和导航星中。

Beside the Funeral Home

Twice a month, I watch special delivery
Of modish coffins for customers anxious
Not to be caught dead in the ordinary

Or to neglect the last public decencies
And thus send parent, aunt or cousin abroad
Again with no mark of comfort or success.

The undertaker's under-men gravely load
Each empty coffin onto a folding cart
And then walk it from the alley to be stowed

Behind a show-room where any broken heart
Costs twelve grand and death looks like a Pontiac,
Chrome -detailed and rust-proofed in every part.

But once cigarettes are stubbed on the sidewalk
And a monk in saffron robe has struck the gong
The cortege is led out by the Cadillac.

Cars reach slowly into traffic and are gone,
A sad departure for these new arrivals,
From a funeral home that calls itself "Wing On."

殡仪馆旁

每月两次我目睹特别运送
为客户所订购的时尚灵柩
为死时不被漠视平凡之辈

或不愿疏忽最后体面离世
因此给海外父母阿姨表亲
送回不顺心不成功的印记

承办随从神情严肃地加载
每个空灵柩到折叠拖车里
然后步行护送着经过巷子

安置在展室后，心碎在那儿
代价一万二，死如庞蒂亚克
所有环节除尘防锈精心处理

而一旦香烟掐灭在人行道上
藏红花长袍的和尚敲响铜锣
即由凯迪拉克引出队列送葬

车辆缓缓驶入车流渐渐消失，
这些新抵达的，一次伤心离别
源自此殡仪馆：名号为"永安"

from *Dante's* House

A year ago, I was thinking of Miche-
langelo almost daily — *Pietà*
as essence of the only art I seek.

Through a colonnade into *la Santa
Sede*, we enter the thousands-long queue
that winds along the edge of the *Piazza*.

The security men watch for some clue
of malice in our eyes, the frenzied will
to bomb the place or kill a pope; in lieu

of present terror, they solemnly fill
their days with enforcement of a dress code —
no bare knees or shoulders, that dishabille

of being young, foreign, and on the road.
The line goes forward — we are through the door
and to the right the garments that once flowed

in marble from his touch — the young sculptor
could see how things fall, mother and dead son,
the posture of brokenness. There is no more

difference among grief, beauty and the stone
though a power to bless remains. It is what
I came for. The press of bodies moves us on.

但丁之居节选

一年前，几乎每天我都想着
米开朗基罗：圣母怜子雕像
为我寻求的唯一艺术精髓。

穿过罗马教廷的庞大柱廊，
我们进入千人排队的长龙
一圈一圈沿着广场的边缘。

保安严密地监视细微线索：
眼中的恶意企图，轰炸这里
或谋害教皇等疯狂念头；鉴于

当前恐怖形势，他们谨慎执行
岗位制度和严格的着装规范 ——
不能裸露膝盖或肩膀，那便装

凸显稚嫩，外籍，以及风尘扑扑。
长龙缓缓前进——我们正通过门廊
到达右厢，那大理石衣衫曾经

随着他的手波动 ——年轻的雕刻家
看到事物如何倾塌，圣母和丧子，
破碎的姿势。悲伤，美丽以及石雕

相融为一体，不再存在任何差别，
而保佑的力量仍然存在。这正是
我来的原因。队伍催促我们向前。

Salve

In Italy, the buildings are for beauty,
and beauty, says Joseph Brodsky, is the enemy
of a hostile world. "Salve," says the customs man
when he stamps my passport.
Which means, "Hello." With the *ve*
jutting out its lower lip. *Salve*, at the bar.
And in the chapel built by plague survivors,
salve, says the cupola. *Salve*, says the floor.
In the Giovanni and Paolo hospital
the old wing opens out like fields and windows
in a Van Gogh painting, light penetrating halls
and making space in silence. No one's there at all,
but — *salve, salve, salve, salve.*
When I return to my more brutal realms
the word comes with me. I don't declare it.
How light in my suitcase it is, how old-fashioned
and almost ethereal, but in some lights
real, and close enough — to salvage.

罗纳•波伦

Salve

在意大利，建筑是为了弘扬美，
约瑟夫布罗德斯基说道，美是
充满敌意世界的冤家。"Salve"
海关人员给我护照盖章时说，
这意味着"你好"当发声时将ve
突出下唇。"你好"，在酒吧。
在瘟疫幸存者建造的小教堂里，
圆顶说"你好"。地板说"你好"。
在乔瓦尼和保罗医院里
破旧的厢房敞开像梵高画里的
田野和窗户，光线透过大厅
并在寂静中留下空间。其实没有人在那里，
但是——"你好"，"你好"，"你好"。。。
当我回到更残酷的境界里
这个词伴我一起。我没有申报它。
它在行李箱里很轻，很老套
几乎空灵，但在某些灯光下
真实，足够接近——获救。

注：Salve 英文有药膏，抚慰的含义，意大利语则
是"hello"（你好）

Bitter Bread

You prepare a feast of bitter bread,
of acid wine and rancid flesh,
then sit me down. Now eat, you hiss,
Eat well of the wrongs that you did to me,
now chomp these chunks, now stuff them in!

I will — I say — but not alone.
Pull up a chair. It's not only I
who must gorge till I'm sick,
till the rank meal's done.

For in love, you must know,
the meat of revenge
is the vengeful's bone,
the dregs of its wine
the avenger's sop.

And the bread that is thrust
on the one who has erred
in matters of love
must always be shared.

苦情面包

你备好一席苦情面包,
酸酒和臭肉的盛宴,
然后要我坐下。现在吃,你嘶语,
好好享受你对我的过失,
现在切碎这些肉块,现在吞塞它们!

我会——我说,但不是独自。
拔出一把椅子。这不是只我
一个人必须狼吞到恶心,
到满桌空倾。

因为在爱情里,你必须知道,
那复仇的肉
是仇恨者的骨头,
酒水的残渣,
复仇者的碎面包。

并且这被推向
爱情中出错一方
的面包
必须始终一起分享。

From the U.S. and elsewhere

来自美国和其他国度

In the Attic

Even though we know now
your clothes will never
be needed, we keep them,
upstairs in a locked trunk.

Sometimes I kneel there
touching them, trying to relive
time you wore them, to catch
the actual shape of arm and wrist.

My hands push down
between hollow, invisible sleeves,
hesitate, then take hold
and lift:

a green holiday; a red christening;
all your unfinished lives
fading through dark summers
entering my head as dust.

安德鲁·姆辛（英国）

在阁楼里

即使我们知道现在
你的衣衫不再
需要，我们还是好好留存，
在阁楼上一个锁好的箱子里。

有些时候我跪在那里
触摸它们，试图去复活
你穿上它们的时光，去捕捉
那臂和腕的真实状态。

我的手向下推向
空心的，无形的袖筒，
迟疑着，然后紧握住
并提起：

一个绿色的假日；一次红色的洗礼；
所有你未完成的生活点滴
在晦暗的夏天里褪去
像灰尘一样进入我的脑海。

The Mistake

The mistake was light and easy in my hand,
A seed meant to be borne upon the wind.
I did not have to bury it or throw,
Just open up my hand and let it go.

The mistake was dry and small and without weight,
A breeze quickly snatched it from my sight,
And even had I wanted to prevent,
Nobody could tell me where it went.

I did not think on the mistake again,
Until the spring came, soft, and full of rain,
And in the yard such dandelions grew
That bloomed and closed, and opened up, and blew.

过失

过失在我的手里简单轻巧，
像种子注定要在风中萌芽。
我并不需把它埋葬或抛高，
只要打开手心并学会放手。

过失干枯细小又没有份量，
微风迅速从我视线中抢走，
即使我曾经想过要去预防，
也无人告诉我它去往何方。

我不再去细想那一次过失，
直到春来，温柔且绵绵细雨，
院子里，蒲公英不断冒出头，
开了又谢，然后再开，并且吹走。

until words turn to moss

This was all roses, here, where an overblown house crowns
the hill, the whole field, roses, all the way to the end;
when the rosarian died, the partition of roses
began. We've come out of nowhere, literally,
nowhere, autumnal towns marked for destruction
by a phantom hand; houses held underwater, every bed
a sunken tub, tools drowned between rows, every keyhole
caulked; clouds hallucinating girls asleep on a wedge
of wedding cake; the white rose, among the greatest of liars
beginning to show the debilitating effects of fame,
the ever-popular blaze placates a vase; the bad sons
of thunder beating back a strand of light; someone
who knows nothing apart from the rain
standing on a chair in muddy legs; the roses
blown into their cumulonimbuses,
and someone whose glove is recovered, a face
that doesn't come clear, a face drawn under an umbrella,
beautiful, charcoal, beautiful, like words
that never get old, the sons of thunder beating

直到文字变成苔藓

这里曾经玫瑰遍地，整个田野和山岗
都是。从山顶上一所鲜花茂密的房子
开始，一路铺展开来。当花匠死去，花儿
开始分离。我们不知出自何方，确实，
不知何方，秋天的小镇已被一只
幻影之手作上毁灭的记号，房屋都没在水中，
每张床一个浴缸，工具淹在花行里，每个洞眼
充塞着；云朵幻象成昏睡于婚礼蛋糕片上的女孩们。
白玫瑰，倍受青睐的光芒抚慰花瓶，于伟大的谎言中
开始败露名望的衰弱影响；雷电的
不肖子击退一缕光，某人
除了雨，毫不知情地
站在椅子上，腿部泥泞，那些玫瑰
被吹进她们的积雨云，
某人找到了她的手套，她的脸
看不清楚，闪在一张伞下，
美丽的，黑炭似的，美丽的，象语言
从来不会变老，雷电的儿子们击打

in our only time

"Follow me," the voice, the long, longed-for voice stops
the writing hand. "I have your shoes." Except
for a rotating fan, movement at a minimum. The plan,
if one can call it a plan, is to begin in what is known
to some as the perennial present; beginning
with a few sentences written in a kitchen while others
cling to their own images in twisted sheets of heat.
A napkin floats from a counter in lieu of a letter. Portals
of the back life part in silence: O verge
of song, O big eyelets of daylight. Leaving milk and bowl
on the table, leaving the house discalced. All this
mystery, mildly erotic. Even if one is terrified
of both death and the color red. Even if a message is sent
each of us in secrecy, no one can make it stay.
Notwithstanding scale — everything has its meaning,
every thing matters; no one a means every one an end

在我们唯一的时间里

"随我来",声音传来,悠长而期盼着的;
"我带上了你的鞋。"让书写的手停了下来。
除了最小风量旋转的风扇。这样的计划,
如果可以算是计划的话,是始于某些已知的
习以为常的礼物,从厨房里写下的几行字开始,
当他人还卷缩在床单余热里想象。
一片餐巾纸飘离台面,取代了一封信。
过往生活的门户默默分隔:
哦,那些歌的尽头,大孔眼的日光。
放下牛奶和碗在桌上,赤着脚离开房子。
这一切的神秘,和暧昧。
即使一个人惧怕死神和鲜红,即使
消息秘密地发送于我们,没有人能让它留下。
尽管衡量,事事有意义,事事有关联;
没有人只是一个过客,每个人都是一个结局

only the crossing counts.

It's not how we leave one's life. How go off
the air. You never know do you. You think you're ready
for anything; then it happens, and you're not. You're really
not. The genesis of an ending, nothing
but a feeling, a slow movement, the dusting
of furniture with a remnant of the revenant's shirt.
Seeing the candles sink in their sockets; we turn
away, yet the music never quits. The fire kisses our face.
O phthsis, o lotharian dead eye, no longer
will you gaze on the baize of the billiard table. No more
Shooting butter dishes out of the sky. Scattering light.
Between snatches of poetry and penitence you left
the brumal wood of men and women. Snow drove
the butterflies home. You must know
How it goes, known all along what to expect,
sooner or later … the faded cadence of anonymity.
Frankly my dear, frankly my dear, frankly

只有穿越重要。

这不是我们如何告别此生，如何从此消逝。
你永远都不会知道，对吧。你以为可以面对
一切。然后它发生了，你却没准备好。你真的
没有准备好。起源的一个结局，空空
只有一个感觉，一个慢动作，亡灵衣衫
的碎片拂拭着家私。
看着蜡烛沉落，我们转过脸去，音乐还在
萦绕。火焰舔着我们的脸。
哦，这只病态的，懒汉的死眼睛，
你不能再凝视台球桌面的绿绒了吧。 不再
射击空中的飞碟。散发光亮。
在诗歌的残片和忏悔之间，你留下
冬日秃林的男男女女。雪把蝴蝶们
赶回了家。你必须知道
事情怎么样，早知道一切后果，
迟或早。。。这无名的旋律归于沉寂。
Frankly我亲爱的，Frankly我亲爱的，Frankly

CALLY CONAN-DAVES

Strife

All contrary noises in the world,
the bang of unlatched things,
the scratching in the wall,
the scrape of nails, the startling of birds
in the long grass —
I shake loose with them.
I am a child, I blaze along the error —
the wrong note struck
when playing a duet,
the china tea set smashed
at Grandpa's house in Sydney,
exciting the scolding chorus,
the stinging smacks — and oh,
it makes bright sound
to get beyond the prudence of forgive me,
to rattle stolen marbles in the tin,
stay outside and shriek when summer thunders,
the glory of all noise against the will
of cautious voices warning calm, keep calm …
I am unsound, the language you were made in,
the silence of a catastrophic breaking.

抗衡

世上所有对立的噪声，
开锁的砰声，
墙上的抓挠，
指甲的刮削，从高高的
草丛里传来鸟的骚动——
我与它们一起摇晃。
我是一个孩子，冒失中燃烧——
双簧表演中
陷入错误的音符，
悉尼外婆家
骨瓷茶具的碎裂，
激起责骂合声，
刺痛的掌击，哦，
多么响亮
远远超出原谅我的那份谨慎，
让锡盒里偷来的弹子嘎嘎作响。
夏天打雷时呆在外面并且尖叫，
所有噪声的辉煌对抗着
那警告安静的谨慎声音的意愿，保持安静。。。
我是靠不住的，你被塑造的语言，
灾难性破坏的沉默。

Do Not Expect

Do not expect that if your book falls open
to a certain page, that any phrase
you read will make a difference today,
or that the voices you might overhear
when the wind moves through the yellow-green
and golden tent of autumn, speak to you.

Things ripen or go dry. Light plays on the
dark surface of the lake. Each afternoon
your shadow walks beside you on the wall,
and the days stay long and heavy underneath
the distant rumor of the harvest. One
more summer gone,
and one way or another you survive,
dull or regretful, never learning that
nothing is hidden in the obvious
changes of the world, that even the dim
reflection of the sun on tall, dry grass
is more than you will ever understand.

And only briefly then
you touch, you see, you press against
the surface of impenetrable things.

不要指望

不要指望假如你的书落下
打开某个特定的页面，你
读到的只言片语一定改变今天，
或者轻风吹过色彩斑斓的
帷幕下的秋天，你正好
偷听到的声音在向你述说。

总有事物成熟或风干。光戏谑
在湖的阴暗表面。每天下午
在墙上你的影子走在你左右，
而在丰收的远道传闻下
日子更加漫长沉重。
又一个夏天过去，
这样或者那样活着，
单调或者遗憾，从未学会
没有什么可以隐藏在
世界的显着变化中，即使是
映射在高高的干草上的昏暗阳光
也比你能明白的更多。

并且仅仅片刻之后
你触到，你看到，你推挡
难以穿透的的事物的表面。

Prayer

Echo of the clocktower, footstep
in the alleyway, sweep
of the wind sifting the leaves.

Jeweller of the spiderweb, connoisseur
of autumn's opulence, blade of lightning
harvesting the sky.

Keeper of the small gate, choreographer
of entrances and exits, midnight
whisper travelling the wires.

Seducer, healer, deity or thief,
I will see you soon enough —
in the shadow of the rainfall,

in the brief violet darkening a sunset —
but until then I pray watch over him
as a mountain guards its covert ore

and the harsh falcon its flightless young.

祷告

钟塔的回声，
小巷的脚步声，
风筛树叶的扫拂声。

蜘蛛网的珠宝商，
秋天丰裕的行家，
收割天空的闪电刀片。

小门的守护者，
出入口的编舞者，
穿越电话线的午夜私语者。

诱惑者，治疗师，神灵或小偷，
我会很快见到你
在雨落下的影子里，

在紫罗兰黯淡日落的短暂时分；
但在那之前，我祈祷守护他
像高山守卫它的隐蔽矿产

和严厉的猎鹰看护无法飞翔的稚鹰。

Thanks for Remembering Us

The flowers sent here by mistake,
signed with a name that no one knew,
are turning bad. What shall we do?
Our neighbor says they're not for her,
and no one has a birthday near.
We should thank someone for the blunder.
Is one of us having an affair?
At first we laugh, and then we wonder.
The iris was the first to die,
enshrouded in its sickly-sweet
and lingering perfume. The roses
fell one petal at a time,
and now the ferns are turning dry.
The room smells like a funeral,
but there they sit, too much at home,
accusing us of some small crime,
like love forgotten, and we can't
throw out a gift we've never owned.

谢谢记得我们

误送到这里的鲜花，
签署着无人知晓的名字，
现在已然凋谢。我们该怎办？
邻居说，花不是送给她的，
附近也没有谁生日临近。
是我们中谁有外遇？
我们理应感谢某人捅这篓子。
起初各自觉得好笑，之后便瞎想。
首先鸣呼的是鸢尾花，
笼罩在其甜得发腻，
久缠不去的浓香里。而玫瑰
每次凋落一片花瓣，
然后现在呢，蕨叶开始干枯。
房间闻起来像极了一次葬礼，
但它们端坐那儿，逍遥自在，
指责我们的一些细微罪行，
比如爱情被遗忘，我们竟不能
扔掉一份不属于自己的礼物。

Turn

The sun's gone to Australia.
The moon's half-hidden face
is facing her from here

and so they see each other
from separate hemispheres.
The earth in love with both

turns in sleep and waking
forsaking nothing ever,
and longing like a river

blindly finds the sea.
And now the leaves are blowing
the grass turns brittle brown,

yet somewhere in Australia
earth is waking now.
The moon's half-hidden face

grows open in the dawn,
the bare trees loose the doves,
the blossoms sway with song.

Everything is dying
even as it lives
and surely as it loves.

轮换

太阳已去澳大利亚。
从这里，月亮半隐藏
的脸对着她

因此相隔半个地球
他们依然看到彼此。
爱着双方的地球

在睡眠和清醒中轮换——
谁也不抛弃，
思念像一条河

盲然地流向大海。
而现在落叶纷飞
草变得脆弱枯黄，

但在澳大利亚某处
地球正在苏醒。
月亮半隐藏的脸

在黎明中敞开，
光秃的枝桠鸽子放飞，
花丛伴着歌儿舞动。

万物在生中也会逝去，
并且一定
爱着也如此。

Lifetime Performance

Don't worry,
this thing is warranted.
When I look at the assembly
of springs and gears
so tentative. Don't worry,
this will be renewed no matter
if it dissociates and even
when the problem can't be found,
someone strong will come, gently
ease me aside, earn my trust,
beat back mysteries, replace parts
and make it run again.

Thinking about repairs
draws the poetry right out of me.
sometimes my life
does just that,
leaving me safe but
eternally uncertain.

终身性能

没什么好担心的，
保险总会有效。
当我看着发条
和齿轮的装配，犹豫不决，
也没什么好担心的。
这些总在不断更新，
即使它分裂甚至
找不出毛病
总会有厉害的人到来，
轻轻推我一旁，
获得我的信任，
驱散神秘，更换零件，
使它重新运转。

联想到修理
这首诗便脱口而出。
有时生活也是如此，
让我有安全感，
但又永远不确定。

Grand Canyon, North Rim

At the edge of a known world
mountains repeat themselves

like old people. Each ripple
a blue syllable, a language of forgetting.

A place like this, exposed
to harsh winters and long years

of drought, begs to be how it was.
I can't but think

standing at the chasm
above the seep willow

how the ghost water raged
like bison through the bottom

of this immense gorge.
Not from flash floods and snow melt,

but a force so powerful
the ground split open, shearing

the canyon raw. What strength could carry
massive boulders miles away?

大峡谷，北缘

在已知世界的边缘
山峦重复自己

像老人一样。每个波纹
一个蓝色音节，一种遗忘语言。

这样一个地方，暴露于
恶劣的冬季和漫长的

干旱，乞求回到当初。
我不能不想到

在沟壑旁
垂柳的上面

幽灵水流如何肆虐
像野牛通过

这大峡谷的底部。
不是来自山洪和积雪融化，

但力量如此强大
使得地面裂开，活生生

劈成峡谷。什么力量可以携带
巨大的石流几英里之远？

Surely no methodical erosion,
but a truth catastrophic

leaving this maw, this mouth
to gawk. My tongue so heavy now

with dust, like a potter's wheel in the sun,
stays mute — having nothing more to say

than two hawks circling the canyon
or the wind coaxing the last leaves

from the cottonwood below.
It's nearly dusk and the red rock face

shifts mood, deepening with itself.
What time changes leaves a shadow,

a human sundial at a precipice. A gnomon
tilted toward a true celestial north.

当然不是有条不紊的侵蚀，
而是一次真正灾难

留下这个鱼肚，这个开口
来瞪视。此刻我的口舌沉重

沾染尘土，就像制陶者的转轮在阳光下
保持安静：没有什么可多说的

除了两只老鹰盘旋在峡谷
或晚风抚弄下边棉木丛

的最后叶片。
已近黄昏，红色岩石

转移着情绪，渐渐深沉。
时间的变化留下它的阴影，

形成悬崖上的一个人工日晷——
指针向真正的天体北方倾斜。

Letter

Tonight, as you walk out
into the stars, or the forest, or the city,
look up
as you must have looked
before love came,
before love went,
before ash was ash.
Look at them: the city's
mists, the winters.
And the moon's glass
you must have held once
in beginning.
That new moon
you must have touched once
in the waters,
saying *change me, change*
me, change me. All I want
is to be more of what I am.

信

今夜，当你离开
步入星空，森林，或者城市，
仰望
就像爱情来临之前，
爱情离去之前，
灰烬化为灰烬之前
你一定也这样望过。
看着它们：这城市的
迷雾，冬日，
以及刚开始时那盏
曾经握在你掌中的
月光杯。
那弯新月
你一定曾经在水中
触摸过，
喃喃自语着：*蜕变我，蜕变*
我，蜕变我。我只想要
做更真实的自己。

A Robin's Nest in Snow

Outside the window of my den
Where I sit usually counting clouds
Or airplanes or chipmunks scurrying by
On a snowy day I still see
The nest through the flurries

Snowflakes are so delicate they melt
On your tongue
Sit proudly
On your shoulders
Tangle themselves
in your braids

Last spring, I didn't know
A bird had made a home
In my river birch
There was activity but I thought
It was the crepe myrtle
Only when the tree exhaled
Did the life reveal itself

The snow piled up neatly
Filling the crevice
Hopefully destroying the viruses and bacteria
That can attack the young still blind robins
And I a survivor of lung cancer nestle
Hope in my heart that no harm will remain
When Spring and birds return

尼克·乔瓦尼

雪中的知更鸟巢

坐在书房靠窗边
我常数天上的云朵，飞机
和树丛中乱窜的花栗鼠
在大雪纷飞的日子，透过飘舞的雪花
我仍然看见那个鸟巢
雪花是那么的微妙，它们融化
在你的舌尖上
潇洒地落在你的肩膀上
并纠缠
在你盘好的麻花辫里

去年春天，我不知晓
一只鸟
在我的河桦树里安了家
那儿有些动静，但我误以为
是绉桃金娘
只有当树枝舒展开来
生命才彰显清晰

冬雪堆积得很齐整
填充着道道隙缝
好希望摧毁那些对稚鸟
具有攻击性的病毒和细菌
我一个肺癌幸存者
在心里筑巢着这样的希望
当春天和鸟雀返回
不会有伤害残存

Time

I dream a lot at night, a lot by day.
Time has no meaning here, where I forget
To mark the hours, where I sometimes let
Whole weeks go wandering freely on their way.

Yet even dreams keep count of moments flying,
When the bolt slides my window and
The bowl of soup is thrust into my hand,
I prolong my life to keep on dying.

Then I discover, shaken from my dream,
How one feels at the end, who has been bound
And set adrift above the thunderous sound

Echoing from Niagara. In midstream
The water hammers at his dinghy's side.
The current surges on. His hands are tied.

R.S.戈温

时间

夜晚我常常做梦，白天也一样。
时间在这儿没有意义，我会忘记
标记钟点，有时更会整周整周地
放任它们无所事事地自由游荡。

只是梦还是把飞逝的时光算记
当我的密室窗口被螺栓栓上，
推塞进我的手里的一碗米汤
让我延长了生命，继续着垂死。

然后颤巍巍地从梦中我发现
一个人临终的感受，那被捆束
并被置于来自尼亚加拉大瀑布

轰鸣之上的漂流的无助。中游处
湍流在他的小艇一侧不断冲击。
激流汹涌。而他的双手被缚系。

Only

After Kunitz

O Love this happened or it did not.
In a room with green walls

my son was born. The cord was torn
too soon, so they cut off

his head to save his heart. He lived
for a long time.

For a long time there was no breath or cry.
When finally he spoke,

he spoke the wide, whorled leaves of corn.
He spoke the crickets

in clusters beneath the sheaves, he sang
the soil in. He sang the wind

in the dune and hush of ebb tide. Some say
he died. Some say he died.

丽贝卡·福斯特

仅此

写在库尼兹之后

哦，爱，这个发生了还是没有。
在一个有绿色墙壁的房间里

我的儿子出生了。脐带撕裂
得太快，所以他们掐断

头来保住心脏。他活了
很长时间。

很长一段时间没有呼吸或哭泣。
当他终于说话时，

他诉说宽阔的，卷起的玉米叶。
他诉说蟋蟀聚集

在稻谷束的下面，他歌唱
泥土。他歌唱沙丘里的风

和退潮的安静。有人说
他死了。有人说他死了。

中诗英译

PART 2

From Chinese to English

初雪

一、

他刚来便又悄然离去
他占领了目光所及的天地以及
灵魂中最玄奥的部位
他静静地躺在众叶之间
躺在早已被人遗忘的水缸里
他降落时浑身颤抖
他蹲在屋脊上却从不以为高人一等
他一向哑默
从不追究为何肤色如此惨白
没有历史，没有轨迹和脚印
翻开去年的照相簿
冷，仍在那里裸着
河水喧哗
是他的笑声，也是挽歌

二、

墙外睡着昨夜的雪
桌上搁着一封未写完的信
我专注地望着
院子里大雪在为一只冻僵的知更鸟
举行葬礼……
我喝着热咖啡
双手奉着杯子搓着，揉着
一直转着
快速地转着

Early Snow

I.

He leaves silently as soon as he arrives
He captures the world where the eyes see
And the soul's most mysterious part
He lies soundlessly among leaves
Lies in a long-forgotten water tank
When he lands, his whole body quivers
High on the roof ridge, never has he thought of being superior
Mute at all times
He has never looked into why skin is so pale
No history, no tracks and footprints,
Opening last year's photo album —
Cold, he is there still naked
The River clamoring ...
It's his laughter, it's also an elegy

II.

Outside the wall, last night's snow sleeps
On the table, an unfinished letter ...
I stare intensely —
In the yard heavy snow is holding
A funeral for a frozen robin ...
I am drinking hot coffee
Hands holding the cup, rubbing,
Continuing spinning
Spinning fast

及至
玻璃窗上的积雪纷纷而落（时钟不停地在消灭自己）

三、

继续写信
非修辞的语调
有点覆雪下败叶的味道
茫然的白，其复杂性
正适于表述一条蛇多次蜕皮的苦心
而且我必须让你知道
从昨夜开始
雪自言自语而来，荒谬如我
虚无亦如
我（时钟不停地在消灭自己）
落雪了……
话未说完他便劈头盖脸地将我掩没
包括毛发、皮肤、指甲
去年拔掉的蛀牙，以及
情绪的蝎子
思想的蟑螂
久久藏于潜意识里的一截毒藤
　　　（时钟，不停地
　　　　在
　　　　消灭自己）

四、

五十年来我第一次被慑住，被蛊惑
　　被一双野性的手猛力拉过来
　　又远远推开
　　这是亘古的一声独白
　　百年孤寂后面
　　还有更多孤寂，更多的百年

176

Until
Snow on the window-glass falls, falls (the clock is constantly
killing itself)

III.

I continue writing the letter
With non-rhetorical tone
It tastes like rotten leaves under the snow
Bemused white, its complexity fits
To express a snake's painstaking shedding over and over
Moreover, I must let you know
From last night
Snow has arrived speaking to himself, ridiculous like me
Void like me
I (the clock is constantly killing itself)
Snow falls…
Before speech finishes, he covers me all over
Encompassing hair, skin, nails
Cavities removed last year, and
Emotional scorpions
Cockroaches of thought
A toxic vine hidden for ages in the subconscious
        (the clock, is constantly
        killing
        itself)

IV.

For the first time in fifty years, I am deterred and deceived
        Pulled over by a pair of wild hands
        Then pushed away again
        This is an ancient monologue
        Behind a Hundred Years of Solitude

我满怀热望而它却极度贪婪
它拒绝了一束玫瑰
却要去了我整座花园
我顿时感到被塑成一个雪人
的悲哀(时钟，
不停地
在消灭自己)
当融化时它将如何忍受
冰水滑过脸部时的那种痒
从史书中翻滚而下那种绝望
一再翻过来穿的
一袭破衲的那种伤心
一些洞洞
瞪视着
另一些洞洞

1997

There is more loneliness, more centuries
I'm full of hope but it's extremely greedy
It has rejected a bunch of roses
But taken my entire garden
I suddenly feel the sorrow of being shaped
like a snowman (the clock,
is constantly
killing itself)
How it will endure when it melts
The kind of itching when ice water slides over the face
The despair that tumbles down from history books
The sadness that wears over and over
Like old worn-out clothing
Some holes
Staring out at
Others

1997

絕句十三帖

第一帖
玫瑰枯萎時才想起被捧著的日子
落葉則習慣在火中沉思

第二帖
所有鮮花都挽救不了鏡中的蒼白
繞到鏡子背後
我看到一堆化石

第三帖
牆上一根釘子有什麼可怕
可怕的是那
釘進去而且生銹的一半

第四帖
夏蟲望著冰塊久久不語
啊，原來只是
一堆會流淚的石頭

第五帖
風息後，蜘蛛忙於修補
那張由別人夢魘織成的網
最後連自己的不幸也織了進去

第六帖
人人每天都要刷牙
而國會麥克風的牙齒從來不刷
任細菌擴散

Thirteen Short Poems

1.

Till withered, roses recall favored days held by caring hands;
fallen leaves get accustomed to meditating in the fire though.

2.

All flowers cannot save paleness in the mirror-
Walking to its back,
I see a pile of fossils.

3.

What horror can a nail in the wall give?
The horrible one is a nail that is half in,
half out, rusted.

4.

Summer worm gazes long at ice cubes -
Ah, they turn out to be
a pile of stones shedding tears ...

5.

We all brush teeth each day
but the teeth of congressional microphones are unbrushed,
left alone to spread germs

6.

Sickened by the filthy air
I wear my skin inside-out
Except for me
people all around whine with aches and pains

第七帖
嫌空氣太髒
我把皮膚翻過來穿
除了我
全世界的人都在喊痛

第八帖
愛情不作興預約
說來就來
蛇咬人從不打招呼

第九帖
擦槍擦了四十年的老班長
於今坐在搖椅上
輕輕地刮著滿身的鐵鏽

第十帖
雨停了
電視裡一場大火燒死了幾個聖人
雨，忽然又下了起來

第十一帖
我在尋找一雙結實的筷子
好把正在沉淪的地球挾起來

第十二帖
一尾被釣起的魚
身在半空仍嘀咕不休：
這是我一生最重要的選擇，可不能出錯

第十三帖
春天真好
萬物各安其生
雀鳥啁啾只不過是蟲子驚叫的回聲

7.

Winds cease; a spider busy playing around
with a web that wove others' nightmares,
finally plaited in its own misfortune.

8.

Love rarely makes any appointment
it just drops in …
Snake bites without a greeting.

9.

Cleaning guns for forty years, the squad leader
sits on a rocking chair
gently scraping the rust that's all over himself

10.

It stopped raining …
On TV, a bonfire burned several saints
suddenly it rains again

11.

I hunt for a pair of powerful chopsticks
to pick up the sinking earth

12.

A caught fish hurled in the air
still murmurs:
This is my life's most important choice,
make no mistake.

13.

Spring is so splendid
all creatures are safe and alive-
birds chirping is nothing but echoes from insects screaming

讀詩十二法

如果我用血寫詩
請讀我以冰鎮過的月光

如果我用火寫詩
請讀我以解凍後的淚水

如果我用春天寫詩
請讀我以最後的一瓣落花

如果我用冰雪寫詩
請讀我以室內的燈火

如果我用濃霧寫詩
請讀我以滿山的清風明月

如果我用泥土寫詩
請讀我以童年淺淺的腳印

如果我用龜裂的大地寫詩
請讀我以豐沛的雨水

如果我用巖石寫詩
請讀我以一條河的走姿

如果我用天空寫詩
請讀我以一只鷹隼的飛旋

如果我用鄉愁寫詩
請讀我以極目無垠的天涯

Twelve Ways of Reading Poetry

If I pump my blood to pen poetry
please read me by icy moonlight

If I burn flame to make poetry
please read me with melting teardrops

If I spend spring to shape poetry
please read me through the final fallen petal

If I blow blizzards for poetry
please read me in your chamber lamplight

If I forge thick fog for poetry
please read me with refreshing winds and the shining moon

If I engrave poetry on clay
please read me with childhood's soft footprints

If I write poetry on parched land
please read me with plentiful cooling rain

If I craft rocks for poetry
please read me with a river's flowing flood

If I apply poetry to the sky
please read me through an eagle's flight

If I muse on nostalgia for poetry
please read me by seeking heaven's canopy

如果我用邪惡寫詩
請讀我以一把淬毒的刀子

如果我用愛意寫詩
請讀我以同一頻率的心跳

If I borrow evils for poetry
please read me with a poisoned knife

If I compose poetry with love
please read me with the same heartbeat

因为风的缘故

昨日我沿着河岸
漫步到
芦苇弯腰喝水的地方
顺便请烟囱
在天空为我写一封长长的信
潦是潦草了些
而我的心意
则明亮亦如你窗前的烛光
稍有暧昧之处
势所难免
因为风的缘故

此信你能否看懂并不重要
重要的是
你务必在雏菊尚未全部凋零之前
赶快发怒，或者发笑
赶快从箱子里找出我那件薄衫子
赶快对镜梳你那又黑又柔的妩媚
然后以整生的爱
点燃一盏灯
我是火
随时可能熄灭
因为风的缘故

Because of the Wind

Yesterday, along the riverbank,
I strolled to the place
where reeds bowed to drink water.
Meanwhile I asked the chimney
to write a lengthy letter in the sky for me
The lines might seem blurred,
But my heart is as bright
as the candlelight by your window.
It is slightly ambiguous,
and inevitably so
because of the wind.

It doesn't matter whether
you understand the letter or not,
what matters is to make sure —
before the daisies haven't wholly withered
you rush to be angry or laugh
rush to find my thin gown in the case
rush to the mirror to comb your black and soft tresses
then with your lifelong love
light the lamp
I am a fire
that might die at any time
because of the wind

歌

谁在远方哭泣呀
为什么那么伤心呀
骑上金马看看去
那是昔日

谁在远方哭泣呀
为什么那么伤心呀
骑上灰马看看去
那是明日

谁在远方哭泣呀
为什么那么伤心呀
骑上白马看看去
那是恋

谁在远方哭泣呀
为什么那么伤心呀
骑上黑马看看去
那是死

1957.2.6.
读里尔克后临摹作

Songs

Who is weeping in the distance?
Why so sad?
Ride on the golden horse to check –
Ah, it is Yesterday.

Who is weeping in the distance?
Why so sad?
Ride on the gray horse to check –
Ah, it is Tomorrow.

Who is weeping in the distance?
Why so sad?
Ride on the white horse to check –
Ah, it is Love.

Who is weeping in the distance?
Why so sad?
Ride on the dark horse to check –
Ah, it is Death.

1957.2.6.
After reading Rilke

蛹

蓦然转身
世界即蜕化成另一种样子
一袭晨衫自你肩际滑落
犹之，鸟之换羽

投出去，迎向虚寂中的虚寂
孤寞中的孤寞
当枨开蝉翼之后，试目
苍山千翠突然汹涌而至
花溢香，鸟歌唱，风走过

极目是千绿万绿无边际的绿
你立其间，锦绣在你掌中

看千浪翻动
托出太阳
犹之你，一伸一握间
抛出一个全然的世界

Pupa

A sudden turn,
the world transforms into another appearance.
Your morning cape slips from your shoulders
as if a bird sheds her feathers.

Casting out, you encounter
the hollow silence among hollow silences
the loneliness among lonelinesses …
Unblocking your see-through wings, you gaze at
one thousand emerald hills suddenly overwhelming;
floral aroma spreads, birds chirp, breezes waft.

In the distance, it is the lavish green and endless green.
You are posed among it, silk brocade in your hands

Watching a myriad of waves
rolling to lift up the morning sun
as if between a grasp and a stretch
you cast out a new world

从双连搭捷运到淡水

我临过帖写过诗的
如今都交付大海了
车子进站的时候
阳光便争相来卡位
世界被压缩成
相扣的铁罐
稍纵即逝的景色

双连相连的车厢
却有不相连的旅程
从起站到终站
多少脸色与眼色交叉而过

前面就是石牌了
牌上究竟镌刻着些什么呢
是我蹉跎
未酬的壮志吗

再下去就是
我挂满笔杆的红树林
那些曾是

到了淡水
竟是终站
太阳已更偏西
我的身影竟抢先去戏水了
淡水不淡
我的愁绪却是越晚越咸
咸到黑发都变灰
变白了

From Double-link to Fresh-water by the Rapid Transit

The calligraphy I copied and poetry I created
now have all been handed over to oceans.
When the train enters a station
the sunlight rushes to jockey for position
The world is compressed into
interlocked tin-cans'
fleeting sight

Although cars are connected from Double-link
they in fact have separated journeys
From a starting point to the end station
How many faces and eyes have met,
then passed by

Ahead it is Stone Plate station.
What exactly has been engraved on the plate?
Are they my hesitant
unfulfilled ambitions?

Continuing again it is
the mangrove forest where I hung up penholders,
full of them, it used to be

When arriving at Fresh-water,
unexpectedly it is the terminal.
The sun clings more to the west
My figure is the first rushing to play with water.
Fresh-water is not fresh
yet my sorrow becomes salty, and saltier
until my black hair turns gray
turns white

碑

那是一张蚀满皱纹的脸
在现实与生存之间
那是一张望着远方发愣的脸

茶壶

一个古老的茶壶
我用今天的开水
泡开一壶陈年的普洱

香槟

我满腹的气
禁不住你一阵摇晃
就冲出口了

情人节

送你
一朵花
然后
把花一瓣一瓣
剥
光

Monument

That is a face full of wrinkles
between reality and survival
that is a face, dazed, gazing into the distance

Tea Pot

an ancient one
I use Today's boiling water
to unwind a pot of age-old Pu-Er

Champagne

my full belly of air
cannot resist your shaking
spurts out from my mouth

Valentine's Day

sending you
a flower
then ...
stripping
one petal
after another

爆米花

我睡着
又实又沉
我醒来
又胖又虚

爆竹

我原本平息的心
都是你
扇风点火
把我气炸了

Popcorn

when sleeping
I am firm and heavy
when awakening
I am puffy and airy

Firecrackers

my restful heart
all by you
ignited with fire and gust
bursting with anger

渡

把自己写进湿冷的诗里
却在你的河岸徜徉
欲描绘一座山的胸臆
测试春水躺在掌心的温度

故事未及布局情节 已滋长青苔
山不动我来 这就是岁月吗
河水悠悠 可承载情迷几许
在人生的长河中 且问
渡过谁的前世
又流向谁的今生

Crossing

I pen myself into these cold and damp poems,
while wandering along your shore;
I long to paint the heart of a mountain
and measure the temperature of spring streams
upheld in your palms.

Before the story develops its plot,
It has already grown green moss.
The mountain sits still; I arrive.
Is this flowing time?
The river unhurriedly runs —
how deep can it carry a love?
In the river of our life, I ask
from whose pre-existence I have crossed
into whose life I now flow.

睡在记忆之上

赤裸而来亦将赤裸而去
且锤炼且挣扎
挤出灵魂最后一滴苦汁
塑生的碑碣在废墟
何谓完善点何谓终站
昨日的落花已随风远飏
今日今日的花尚未含蕾

时间犹似石磨磨着
记忆的芥草
在记忆上睡着
不是我的影子吗?

睡在记忆上
那闪闪的灯
此刻又照见什么
意识理性与欲念

「卑贱人不过是一丝气息,
尊贵人不过是一场幻影,
把他们放在天平上一秤,
比空气还轻,毫无分量。
」(注)
啊!这是谁的声音

阴翳盘桓在心胸
我迷失在零时之后
组空白的梦幻成串
投影于棕榈滩上

Sleeping on Memory

I have come naked and will leave naked too —
being tempered, having struggled
I will squeeze the last drop of the bitter juice from the soul
The plastic monument is in ruins ...
What is the beginning, and what is the ending?
The falling flowers of yesterday have gone with the wind
Today, today's flowers have not yet budded.

Time is like a stone grinder
grinding
the mustard of memory
sleeping on memory —
Isn't it my shadow?

Sleeping on memory
that gleaming lamp
what does it shine on now?
Consciousness, rationality and desire

"Surely men of low degree are vanity,
and men of high degree are a lie:
to be laid in the balance,
*they are altogether lighter than vanity."**
Oh! Whose voice is this?

Tree-shade hovers in my heart
I am lost after midnight
Combining blank fantasy into cords
I cast them on the palm beach

而那里的太阳会否落沉
梦是否曳着光泅来

站着的的影子
在异乡睡在记忆上
我失去重量

注：圣经诗篇62：9

Will the sun there set or not?
Does the dream come wading through light?

Standing, my slender shadow
in a foreign land, sleeping on memory
I have lost gravitas.

    * Note: Bible Psalm 62:9

致在热火中水的呼吸

啊，又退回又退回到这扇门里
它狭窄，幽暗，悲凉，没有呼吸
连空气都被死亡啃噬着

七月流火已扑向门前
这时才想起蛇体的游滑和鱼肢的灵活
它们多么善于和容易逃离现场
而不象那滴水
任火舌将它吞咽

啊，你不要和那滴水一样
把你灵魂里的水汁全都分泌出来
把你死角里的冰山用这火去解冻
你不是那滴不能呼吸的水
你是无穷的源流
足以降压体温之上的火势

时间的狱门必由时间打开
在沦落的精神世界里
滴水的呼吸是你通向清澈的暗道
丢了钥匙，迷了路
只要你心中还有一个地址
不管天昏地黑
总有到达的时候

To the Breath of Water in the Intense Fire

Ah, back, back to the door again
a narrow, dark, sad, unbreathing door
even the air is clutched by death

July's burning fire approaches its front
Only now I recall the slippery snake and nimble fish —
how easily they can flee from the scene
not like the waterdrop —
leaving itself to be swallowed in flames

Ah, do not be like that waterdrop!
Gather all the juice from each part of your soul
Thaw your dead corners' iceberg with the fire
You are not the waterdrop that cannot breathe
You are the infinite head-waters
capable of diminishing this body's fire

The hell of time must be opened by time itself
In the fallen spiritual world
the breathing of your water is
the hidden path to purity
Even with keys lost and ways unknown
as long as there is an address in your heart
Regardless whether faint or gloomy
you will always arrive

时间的声音

有时候我想着但知道
这一刻没有你。……我不确定。

你还在？在我的怀疑中？

高大槐树间阳光的回旋曲
一簇簇卵形的叶子演奏
莫名的凉意。草开始发黄。

老人拄着拐杖走着最后的路。
我在阴影中做白日梦。有时候
我想着并试图感到你
当我的心在泥地里打滚。

又一次到来的秋天，星辰坠落
被痛苦撞醒的时刻 —— 那是你
在我的听觉所能触摸到的
死亡的光头上。

The Sound of Time

Sometimes I think, but know
There isn't you in this moment ...
I am not sure.

Are you still here? in my suspicion?

Among tall acacia trees
clusters of oval leaves play
the sunlight's rondo.
Inexplicable coolness. Grasses turn yellow.

An old man walks with a cane to his last journey.
I daydream under the shades. Sometime
When my heart rolls in the mud
I expect and try to feel you.

Again autumn arrives; stars fall.
The moment I'm woken up by pain —
it is you on death's bald head
where my hearing reaches

废墟

废墟里有着自由那
奇怪的阴影

在徘徊。在咳嗽
清理嗓子

它也迷恋可能的解放
所以，它也赞美。
但是，只赞美高度
在瓦砾和低矮的野草之上

深处的蛇悄悄游动。
盯着无数脚跟的盲目

爬上供品的祭台，花朵枯萎着
这是必然的枯萎。这是
必然的乌鸦驮来了成功者要求的黄昏。

这首诗或许写得太早，但已经太晚——

世界各处都在倒塌
那高大的殿堂。那废墟的主席台
还会重建，因为自由的阴影
在徘徊，咳嗽

在话筒前又开始清理嗓子。

The Ruins

There is that strange shadow
Of freedom in ruins

Wandering, coughing
To clear its throat

It obsesses about the possible liberation
Therefore, it praises too.
But only praises the height
Over the rubble and weeds.

A snake hidden in the depth silently slithers.
Staring at the blind heels of tourists

It climbs up the altar that offers sacrifices; the flowers wither
They inescapably wither. It is
A dusk that the inevitable ravens bring
Upon the request from the successful.

This poem has been probably written too early,
But already too late —

Around the world the tall pillars
Are collapsing. The podium in ruins
Will be rebuilt, because the shadow of freedom
Still wanders, coughs

And begins to clear its throat in front of the microphone

一块石头

一块石头从山岩上滚下
引起了一连串的混乱
小草哎呦喊疼，蚱蜢跳开
蜗牛躲避不及，缩起了头
蝴蝶忙不迭地闪，再闪
小溪被连带着溅起了浪花

石头落入一堆石头之中
——才安顿下来
石头嵌入其他石头当中
最终被泥土和杂草掩埋

很多年以后，我回忆起
童年时代看到的这一幕
才发现这块石头其实
是落入了我的心底

A Rock

A rock rolling down from a stony mountain
causes a chaotic series —
grasses cry out for pain, grasshoppers jump off
snails cannot run away, instantly shrinking
their heads into their shells
butterflies hectically flutter, and flutter again
a creek below is splashed with waves

The rock falls into a mass of boulders
— then it settles down
embeds itself among other rocks
eventually they are buried under mud and weeds

Many years later, I remember seeing
this scene in my childhood:
The rock is found in fact fallen
into the bottom of my heart

山中一夜

恍惚间小兽来敲过我的门
也可能只是在窗口窥探
我眼睛盯着电视，耳里却只闻秋深草虫鸣
当然，更重要的是开着窗
贪婪地呼吸着山间的空气

在山中，万物都会散发自己的气息
万草万木，万泉万水
它们的气息会进入我的肺中
替我清新在都市里蓄积的污浊之气

夜间，缱绻中风声大雨声更大
凌晨醒来时，在枕上倾听的林间溪声
似乎比昨晚更加响亮

A Night in Mountains

In a trance, a little beast knocked on my door;
it might just have peeked out my window.
I was staring at the television, yet what I heard
was only sounds from insects in autumn's deep grasses.
Well, more important was opening the window,
to greedily inhale the fresh air in mountains.

In mountains, every creature spread its own breath —
grasses and trees, springs and rivers …
their breath entered my lungs
helping to clean out the amassed filthy urban air in me.

At night, lying in my bed, I listened to the gust,
rain beating wildly.
In the morning, I woke to hear
the running creek in the woods
sounding event more distinct.

旧巷

触碰旧巷的花草
一种思绪逆流而上
小溪从脑际流过，便有旧种子
往下而落，一丛草迎蜂招蝶

我担心水弄湿裤角
上岸，扔下诱饵
垂钓水潭深处
一头红鲤鱼动弹不得
不知是否被往事下毒

紫荆花香，熏染我辨不清回家路
转眼而逝，一把把红雨伞
一只只白蝴蝶
备有嫁衣，凝成黄色的蛹

月亮捞起路上的灯红
看清漫长的路

Old Lanes

Once I touch flowers and grasses in old lanes,
my thoughts trace back like currents.
A stream crossing my mind, old seeds
descend and drop. A cluster of grass
greets bees and beckons butterflies.

I worry water will soak my pant legs.
So I come ashore, cast the bait
to fish in deep water.
A red carp fails to move,
I wonder if it is poisoned by the bygones.

Cercis' blossoms spread their fragrance,
causing me to lose my way home.
In the blink of an eye, all has gone,
red umbrellas one by one,
white butterflies each with a bridal dress,
congealed in yellow cocoons.

Moon scoops up the red light on the road,
sees its way afar and drawn-out.

社区麻将阵

四条腿的麻将桌当然稳定
小小的明争暗斗之后
洗牌声宣示和谐

也就是一些亲戚和朋友
来此补偿升官发财未了的夙愿
或是一些官场商场的得意和失意者
离退休之后，到此尽未尽的余兴，且
绝对平安，人际关系已简化为东南西北
搏杀只在一平方米的牌桌上
即使付出代价，壮烈牺牲，也只是一些
以"人民"命名的
小金额纸币
而不是你我这些血肉之躯的人民

难得糊涂么？
辽阔深远的天空
已缩减为
头上
一面爬满苍蝇的屋顶

Community Mahjong Array

With four legs, Mahjong tables stand stably
after teeny-tiny open fights or secret strife.
The shuffling sounds declare harmony.

They are just some friends and relatives,
come here to compensate for
their unfulfiled wish of being rich,
or businessmen and politicians,
some who've done well, others failures,
after retirement, come to enjoy and
relax in this completely-safe way that
social relationships have been simplified
to battles of East, West, South and North
on one small square table.
The toll for payback or sacrifice is just
some small face value bills
in the name of the "people",
not people with real flesh and blood like you and me.

It is hard to be muddle-headed?
The vast sky above
has shrunk into
a small roof
crawling with flies.

秋韵

给f.c

飘泊多年，我遗失了
你给我的那颗红豆
只有那温暖的南风
至今还缠绕在心头

走完了炎热的长夏
我进入生命的清秋
细辨沧海桑田
何事是天长地久？

隐隐有丹桂飘香
牵惹我思绪悠悠
举起一只空杯
让明月为我斟酒

时光将携我而去
唯有这杯酒长留
千百代有人品味
当这月明时候

Autumn Poem

To f.c

After many years of wandering,
I lost the red bean you gave to me.
yet the warm breeze from the South
still entwines in my mind.

Walking through a long scorching summer,
I enter into the autumn of life.
Discerning huge changes all the time,
I wonder, "what is eternal?"

Laurel blossoms scent faintly,
bring my mind faraway.
I hold up an empty cup,
beg the full moon to pour me wine.

When time takes me away,
only the wine will last.
While the moon shines through
hundreds and thousands of generations,
someone shall sip the wine.

响起歌声的夜晚

覆盖大地的夜晚向一盏灯合围
它只能把一盏灯围住，却不能把一盏灯变黑

一盏灯挂到多高，成为星星？
一盏灯挂到多高，再也看不到？

在夜晚出行，就像在潜泳
时间越长，潜得越深，就像黑夜
它有一个核心

在夜晚，更象是灵魂的出行
我的眼睛明亮，却什么也看不见
我只看到自己的灵魂和眼睛

只有月光
引领着我们上升 柔柔的清辉照到心灵
带来忧伤 在忧伤的光明中
我听到由远而近的歌声 圆润的歌声
使夜晚变得嘹亮，而又安详

The Night in Which Songs Rise

The shades of night falling upon earth,
envelop a lonely lamp.
Its darkness can circle the lamp, but never dim it.

How high could a lamp be hung up to become a star?
How far could it rise to be out of sight?

To walk into the night is like diving in the water,
the longer you stay, the deeper you dive,
as the dark night has a core inside.

At night as if our soul gets out from us,
my eyes are bright but I see nothing
I only see my own spirit and my eyes.

Only the moonlight leads us to rise,
its soft light is cast on our mind,
and brings the sadness.
In the sorrowful sheen,
I hear songs from far and near,
the mellow singing brightens the night,
loud and clear in peace.

削梨的声音

我独坐灯下削梨
削一个细皮的苍溪鸭梨
水汁直往外汪
皮一圈一圈地掉
但不断。此刻我听见
皮离开水果的声音
均匀如呼吸
更如我的心情
夜深人静。我独坐灯下
倾听削梨的声音

The Sound of Peeling a Pear

I sit alone by a lamp
peeling a pear
a thin-skinned CangXi pear
Juice overflows
Spirals of peel circle down
not yet broken.
Meanwhile I hear
the sound of the skin
parting from the fruit —
easy like breath
more like my mind
in the quiet deep night.
I sit alone by the lamp
listening
to the sound of peeling.

静物

坐在盘子里的苹果，面朝你，浮泛起
静物的宁。你的颜料涂亮我圆润的弧
画家，你能抹平我遥远的痛么
搁在果皮下面、果肉深处。如果追溯
上可追溯遥远的十字花科
两把凶器交叉，控制命脉

我不为难你。只请你午后开窗缝儿，让
那只采蜜归来的蜂，立我的蒂
一如地质学家伏在东非大裂谷，鸟瞰
我伤口的深度

The Still Life

The apple sits on the tray, facing you,
floating a still life's peace.
Your pigment spreads and shines my plump arc;
Painter, can you smooth my remote pain
which lies under the skin, the deep inner pulp?
If traced back, it may trace
the distant cruciferous:
two weapons are crossed to control the lifeline

I do not want to bother you.
Only plead to open the window a crack after noon,
let the bee that returns from nectar picking
stand on my pedestal
and look down the depth of my wound
as if a geologist bending over The Great Rift Valley.

从唐朝到江南

我一身富贵
随手就是唐朝
丢下李白
他喝醉了
今夜长安无眠

你品茶江南
抬眼满是桃花
挟着香风
我匆忙寻你
今夜紫禁茫然

千年,白衣只轻轻一飘耳

水和梦就漫过月光屋顶
时光之足湿遍

From the Tang Dynasty
to the South of the Yangtze River

Wealthy as I am,
I carry
the whole Tang Dynasty,
dropping off Li Po
who was drunk –
Chang-An City, tonight, is sleepless.

You sip tea to the south
of the Yangtze River;
looking up, eyes full of peach blossom.
Among the fragrant breezes,
in haste, I search for you –
the Forbidden City, tonight, at a loss

Ah, a thousand years pass swiftly as a white garment flies by

Streams and dreams overflow the moonlit roof,
time's feet are drenched

李广田

笑的种子

把一粒笑的种子
深深地种在心底，
纵是块忧郁的土地，
也滋长了这一粒种子。

笑的种子发了芽，
笑的种子又开了花，
花开在颤着的树叶里，
也开在路旁的浅草里。

尖塔的十字架上
开着笑的花，
飘在天空的白云里
也开着笑的花。

播种者现在何所呢，
那个流浪的小孩子？
永记得你那偶然的笑，
虽然不知道你的名字。

LI GUANG TIAN

A Smile Seed

Someone brings a smile seed,
plants it deeply in my heart.
Even though it's a sad land,
it still grows this smile seed.

The smile seed sprouts.
The smile seed blooms
among the trembling leaves,
and in grasses by roadsides.

On the cross at the steeple
there are smiling flowers.
Amid white clouds in the sky
there are smiling flowers as well.

Where is the sower now,
that wandering child?
I have forever remembered your smile,
though I don't know what your name is.

林静

冬日

开始了
冷酷的寒风
似乎永不懂得停歇
而野蛮者和他冥顽的游戏
依然放纵在大地上

江河早已冻结
饥饿掀起的
骚动
阵阵
抖驱着昨日的默然

梦的天空中
寒霜沉结成星星
荒凉的峡谷里
主宰者
是那被扭曲了的古老的传说

永远无法改变
陷井里的一切
谎言
一次又一次地撒响
戏弄着
被封锁了的饥馑的大地和漫长的苦难

Winter Day

It begins.
Cold chilly winds
seem to never know stopping,
as the brute and his cruel games
oppress the earth.

Rivers are already frozen.
Hunger surges consistently,
agitating yesterday's muteness.

In the sky of all dreams,
bleak frosts cohere into stars.
Beyond remote valleys,
the dictator is the twisted old legend.

Things in traps never change.
Lies like sirens blare again and again,
teasing
the sealed starving earth
and longg sufferings.

蔡利华

月光和湖边的变奏

"人生是一张单程车票"，你说话时
月亮已从树丛里飘出，星星在远天闪烁
你拨响水面，眼神凝重深沉
风滞留在树枝上，山峰向月色退去

我似是而非的向水中游去
铁黑的水从我手背流向上方
我不想说明，我弯弯的山路已经千折百回
月光下闪烁古老的生命，黑暗中树叶有声的和鸣
湖上银光潋滟，都在心中回荡今夜的热情
我相信生命没有同一时刻，今晚的风
不再有相同的轨迹

我迎接你的目光，如月色刺穿忧伤
我们漫步月色下的小径，看银杏树瀑布般的繁枝
托起明净的沧月，把湖面变成今夜的辉煌
我说：我要离开这样的美丽
你举目远方，你无意从我心中捕捉和谐的语言

The Variation of Moonlight and the Lake

"Life is a one-way journey."
When you say that,
the moon floats out from trees,
stars glimmer far away.
You strike waves on the lake,
solemn and sad in your eyes
The wind halts on branches,
mountain summits fade away.

I swim dreamily to the center of the lake.
Dark streams flow up the back of my hand.
I cannot explain —
my path has been curved and hidden,
while ancient life still shines under the moon,
leaves rustle in the dark,
ripples resonate with tonight's passion ...
I believe there is no single moment
the same as tonight
and the wind will never have the same path.

I meet your staring, as sorrowful
as the piercing moonlight.
We wander under the moon
and watch the lush branches
of the ginkgo tree cradle the bright moon.
We watch the growing glory of tonight's lake.
I say to you, "I will leave such beauty behind."
You gaze faraway, fail to capture my deep meaning.

很久以后，我又回到湖边，当我想起你时
我心中又有了那一轮月亮，微风依然，只是两鬓寒霜
古老的银杏还在那一片沧月里，确认我不变的信仰
还有我平凡的人生，不再有你的目光照耀
你的面容就在那个月夜流进了我永久的诗行。

Years later,
I will be back here again.
When I think of you,
the same moon will rise in my heart.
The breeze will still blow;
yet my hair will turn grey.
The old ginkgo tree will witness
my unchanged faith and my ordinary life.
Though your illumination may not stay,
your face is carved eternally
in my poem since this night.

渴望的房间

有那么多奢侈的情绪
在随意打发的日子中积累
空洞的回声弹来弹去
窗是愿望，墙是氛围

我们画出了门的位置
过多的设计，使事实神秘
永远的门，是永远的平面
我们虚弱的立体，无法穿越

我们责备自己，回避问题
而窗户是悲剧的真正中心
风景拥挤进来，房间正填为固体
使我们不能呼吸，不能出去

The Room of Desire

So many excessive emotions accumulated
in our days of random spending
The empty echo bounced back and forth
The window was the wish, the wall was the atmosphere

We drew the location of the door
Too much design made the facts mysterious
The forever door was the forever plane —
our fragile three-dimensions, unable to pass through

We blamed ourselves and avoided problems
but the window was the tragedy's true center
Scenes squeezed in and the room was filled solidly —
we couldn't breathe, couldn't escape.

中东

沙漠里长大的一对小小的兄弟，
在母亲的枕边听说过
傍晚瓶子里升起的风暴，
但从未看清你手中散发着青烟的枪口。

子弹在他们稚嫩的形体内
打出了两口深井，
但让你失望的是，喷涌出来的不是石油
而只是血的逃亡的碎片。

那是他们给你的最后的问候。
你赢了。你砍掉了
两个梦的提案，像是锄掉了
你在犹他州的院子里的两株杂草。

远处，被声浪洗刷的村舍。
更多的奶嘴和围兜在震撼与敬畏中醒来。

如果我用悲哀锁上自己的眼睛，
你可不可以现在
就将准星从他们的胸口移开，
让他们按自己的计划喧闹地长大？

注："逃亡的碎片"是加拿大女作家安妮·麦克尔斯的小说名

Middle East

Two little brothers growing up in the desert
heard from their mother's knee that
storms rise at dusk from the bottle,
but they never made out the muzzle's blue smoke in your hands.

Bullets in their young bodies
drilled two deep wells,
But to your disappointment, it was not oil pouring out
but bloody fugitive pieces.

They were their last greetings to you.
You won. You have cut off
the two proposed dreams just like
getting rid of two weeds in your yard in Utah,

In the distance, villages were washed by sound waves.
More pacifiers and bibs were wakened up in shock and awe.

Brother, If I squeeze my eyes shut with sorrow,
Can you now
move the crosshairs off their chests
and let them grow up noisily as they have planned?

note: *Fugitive Pieces* is a novel by Anne Michaels

穿越

我把两本印着敌对思想的书
并排放在硬木书架上。

一样的文字，有着无可辩驳的亲缘的词语
在不同的立场上互致着怀疑和敌意。

夜里，书架上传来怨恨的噬咬声，
不知是词语之间，还是词语和牙齿的遭遇。

我用一张塑料纸把二者审慎地分开，
它们才渐渐安静，像一场决斗后留下的两块碑文。

三年后，当我再从架上取下其中一本，
我发现薄膜的两面嵌着来自双方的文字残迹。

就像一块琥珀，封存着它们向彼此穿越的企图、
临终的挣扎，直到目光的熄灭，

但我无法断定，那是边境线上心照不宣的渗透，
一场失败的叛逃，还是一次冒死的亲近。

Passing

I placed two books that printed hostile thoughts
side by side on a hardwood bookshelf.

The same language, words with undeniable kinship
sent each other distrust and dislike from dissimilar angles.

At night, I heard the bites of resentment from the shelf.
I wondered if those were made by the words themselves or teeth.

Only after I separated the two with a piece of plastic,
did they quieten down, like two epitaphs after a deadly duel.

Three years later, when I took one down from the shelf,
I found bits of text embedded in both sides of the plastic.

It was like amber sealing their efforts to pass through,
their final struggles until the light left the eyes.

But I could not tell if it was an undeclared border infiltration,
a failed defection, or a death-defying reunion.

服刑

我们一出生就是为了和时光诀别
只是苟且于缓刑

而罪名
早已被印在了判决书，只是你只能
一天翻阅一页
直到阅尽千帆，阅尽世微
阅完最后一个句号
你方能，俯首签字
是否膺服

你无期是役为匠
在囚禁你的花圃，修剪你的刑期
你栉风沐雨，劬劳辛苦
一寸一寸地，为自己减刑
你最终，剪到了
泥土

Serve a Sentence

born to say goodbye to time
we drift along
with probation

but our sins
have been printed on the verdict
and you only can
turn one page a day
until after a thousand sailings
until grasping each grain of sand
until the last period is read
then you can bow down and sign
whether to accept it

serving for a lifetime like a gardener
you prune your sentence in a garden
that imprisons you:
with winds combing your hair
and rains washing your face
you take all the toil -
inch by inch, shortening the sentence
finally, paring it
  down to
    the soil

若蓝天可以打包

午后在家附近湖边漫步
一袭长长羽绒衣
也不能将瑟瑟的冷
走成局外

湖面被冰层冷冻
凝望头顶那蓝得化不开的
苍穹，怀忧万里之遥
被雾霾缠身的众生

如果蓝天可以打包下载
我该输入哪一个邮址
才不是一句自作多情的
笑语

If the Blue Sky Could be Packed up

After noon I took a long stroll
by the lake near my home
Wearing a prolonged winter-coat
I kept walking - walking, yet
the chill refused to leave me alone

The lake, covered by ice, frozen ...
Above my head, the blue sky
so blue, I gazed at its immensity
but my heart full of worries
about all beings being entangled
in the smog afar

If the blue sky could be downloaded
as a package
which address should I add to send —
so not to be laughed at as
this useless compassion?

相信

相信——是不可能造就可能的
一程芬芳，是可能断送
不可能的一缕萌芽

相信——一滴泪不汇入大海
也能掀起一片涛声
而灯光倾其一生柔情
也无法将窗外的夜色照亮

相信——夜深不是因为钟摆指向
人静不是因为三缄其口
生命之船，有时
不是遇上暗礁才会掉头

相信每一次思想之上的扬帆
都是心灵的展翅回归

Believe

Believe — it is the impossible that makes a possible
sweet-scented journey; it is the possible that ruins
an impossible sprout

Believe — a tear not flowing into the sea
can also make waves
and a light expending its full softness
still cannot light up the night sky
outside the window

Believe — night is deep not because a clock pendulum points ...
people grow quiet not because of being shut up
the life boat, sometimes
turns around not just to avoid rocks

Believe — the sailing beyond each thought
is the return of the winged soul

PART 3

Poems Inspired by translations

译者之意外收获

The Great Cold

after translating Luo Fu's Early Snow

How to take the loneliness?
How to pass the long night?
To your back, the distance was blurry...
silent again.
I wish I'd be at your side
listening to you...or reading your letter,
I wish time would not pass by:
Like love held by hands,
like the frozen robin being alive ...

Yet snow falls
far and near
on me
on   me

大寒

翻译洛夫的《初雪》有感

如何承受那无边的孤独?
如何度过那漫长的黑夜?
在您身后，远处一片苍茫。。。
一再沉默。
但愿我在您身边
倾听您…或者读您的信，
但愿时间不会流逝——
就像爱握住了，
就像冻僵的知更鸟又复活了。。。

而雪，不断落下
在远处，在身上。

A Dream

after translating Al Moritz's poems

Into a forest,
you follow a sound.
The child you are,
searches for seeds of passion fruit;
instead, leaves of autumn fall over you.
Their rich colors
make a maze of wonderland.
Picking up one and another,
you see a map of lost memories.
Each drop of yesterday,
each light of moon and sun,
sweet and sad, suddenly you grow up.
On the autumn mirror, the
sparkling moving new world
that you have stepped in,
your fingertips slip into,
spinning shining stars …
The child you are, the child you are not,
scoop up,
the sweetness,
the song of a heart,
calling
to awake …
the child you are,
the child I am.

梦

翻译阿尔伯特·莫里茨有感

随着一种声音，
你踏入林中。
童真的你，
遍寻百香果的种子。
秋天落满你一身枫叶：
它们丰满的色彩
铺成迷宫般的仙境。
一片一片拾起，
通往记忆的地图一一浮现：
每一瓣昨天，
每一道月亮和太阳的光亮，
甜蜜而忧伤，
突然间你长大了。
在秋天的镜子上，这个流动的
闪闪发光的新世界，
你的指尖滑入，
旋转再旋转，
那些闪亮的星星。。。
你是那孩子，你又不是那孩子，
舀起来，
那些甜蜜，
那来自心灵的声音，
召唤
每一次醒来。。。
你是那孩子，
那孩子是我。

255

Late Trains

In our last call we talked about weather.
Spring is finally here and I forgave the long winter.
I intended not to mention those cold nights —
I moon-watered your poems.
They flowed into my veins, softening
my snow-buried garden ...
No point to worry you,
I remarked that the wintersweet bloomed
... I could send you some shoots.

We two are orphans.
I remember a precious diary given to me
for my eighteenth birthday, so delicate and exquisite.
I wrote in it and saved it for you.
My handwriting still hasn't become better;
my best poems haven't arrived.
The diary grew out-of-date and eventually was lost.

Our call ended with Mary Oliver's line,
poems are ropes to let down for the lost ...

Outside my window, night trains
come and go. I catch shadows
of wings that only soar in dreams.

夜行的列车

最后一次通话，
我们谈到天气，谈到风景。
春天终于来了，
我开始原谅漫长的冬季，
并且刻意不提到——
那些寒冷的日子，诗来取暖。
我轻描淡写另一个时区
红梅也许开放。

我们都是孤儿。
记得18岁生日收到一本日记
如此精致和美丽，
我写下了手记，只为你保留。
然而，我的笔迹没有变得更好，
我的诗也没能更成熟，
于是日记一直封装着，最终丢失。

诗是绳索，为失落者放下来。。。
我们的通话以玛丽.奥利弗的诗句结束。

窗外，火车来了又去。
我瞥见带翅膀的影子，
那些羽毛只在梦中翱翔。

Lucky Days

after Marty Gervais and *Bruce Meyer*

They call you
a lucky girl.
Nobody knows
you are careful
to pinch
your own luck
— not too much of it,
or else you must fall in the dark.

You often dream of a black cat
but wake up to catch
a glimpse of yourself —
irises so bright,
eager to jump out.

You admit your blessing —
to retreat to shadows in time ...
turning into a shadow maker,
not a moth toward fire.

The unknown remains unknown.
Sirens shatter Gwendolyn's dream.
With luck, a life you know —
the way of Poetry.

Note: *Shadow Maker* is the title of Rosemary Sullivan's Life of
poet Gwendolyn MacEwen

幸运日子

——读马缇·爵威和布鲁斯·迈耶

他们唤你
幸运的女孩。
没人知道
你很小心
拿捏自己的运气。
——不要太多，
不然会跌入黑暗。

你经常梦见
一只黑色的猫
但醒来瞥见
自己的身影——
眼睛闪亮，
急于跳出。

必须承认你的幸运——
及时撤退到阴影中。。。
一个影子制造商，
而不是飞蛾
去满足扑火的辉煌。

未知仍然保持未知。
警报器粉碎了格温多林的美梦。
幸运的是，你的生活，自己清楚——
以诗歌的方式。

In Duplicate

Beware of things in duplicate
—Dana Gioia

These days you read for signs:
on a table, a set of blue china,
at the window, a spider's web ...
Over your head, a floating cloud,
shape hard to name,
then a sudden gust — hot and salty —
from the east or west?

You sleepwalk in a maze.
Nothing is lost.
The book you hold in red and gold
conceals blue:
Do not expect that you have left
threads in others' dreams.
The maze disguises its green exit.

Everything you hold — so small —
still hurts when not returned;
you wish to duplicate it:
keys, hands, hearts, and love ...
For if a mistake is made,
then you, at least,
have another
to hold.

一式两份

当心重复的事物
　　　——达纳·乔依尔

这几天你沉迷迹象：
桌上，一套蓝色的瓷器，
窗边，一个空蜘蛛网。
头顶，一朵浮云，
外形无法命名，
而一阵风过———咸热———
来自东方或西方？

你在睡眠中行走迷宫。
东西没有丢失。
你手里的红色和金色的书，
隐藏着蓝：
不要指望你会
在别人的梦里留下线索。
迷宫掩盖着的绿色出口。

你持有的一切———虽然小———
但无法返回仍然會悲傷。
你想复制它们：
钥匙，指针，心肝和爱。
因为如果出错一次，
那么爱人，至少，
还有另外一份
可以拥持。

To Molly Peacock

Before I met you
I dreamt of a pink peacock
in a foreign land with the foreign language
spreading splendid feathers.

Yet the peach remains a dilemma,
No wonder Prufrock wandered,
longing to decide,
and for you, a red tinge, with a hinge
to a renewed world.

Make it new, I heard,
both of you claim.
Now I look at leaves and fruits,
stones and stars, each a new poem.
I too bite the juicy fruit of it.

致莫莉.皮克

在遇见你之前
我梦见一尾粉色的孔雀
在异国用异域的语言
美丽地开屏。

而蜜桃仍是一个难题
难怪普鲁弗洛克徘徊,
渴望着决定,
而于你,桃红的一点承接着
进入一个更新的世界。

我听到,让它变新
你们都声称。
现在我看着叶子和果实,
石子和星辰,每一个
都是一首新诗。我也
咬到了它多汁的果实。

Spirit Tree

after Priscila Uppal

In Prospect Cemetery,
among poplar, cedar and maple trees,
I hope you found yours —
the healing from heaven.

Here in another city,
from my window,
I can see a full-grown willow —
ten years ago, only a tiny twig
someone dropped in the valley.

I remember two years ago,
the year you passed, lightning
hit the willow and split her into halves.
I worried and almost let go,
but the next year,
from the open wound,
she grew new twigs.

Have I found my spirit tree?
I trek every day …
Last year, when I passed by the willow,
the breeze blew — new green leaves
touched me as if a soft hand.

When winter comes,
I collect all fallen slim leaves,
so much like lips.

灵树

——读佩瑟丽·阿帕的同题诗

在展望公墓，
柏杨，雪松和枫树之间，
我期望你找到属于你的——
来自上天的愈合。

这儿另一城市里，
从窗口望去，
我可以看到一棵高大的柳树——
十年前，只是小柳枝，
某人随手弃于山谷边。

我记得两年前-
你离去的那年，闪电
击中柳树，劈成两半。
我好一阵担心，几乎
放弃了，可是来年
敞开的伤口处，
新的柳枝又冒出了。

我可找到自己的灵树？
每天跋涉着…
去年，当我路过柳树时，
微风吹来——新绿的柳条
轻抚我——仿佛柔软的小手。

冬天来临，
我收集所有飘落的柳叶，
片片好像微闭的嘴唇。

I let them rest in books
of poems by you,
each clinging to another
whispering a forest of stories.

我把她们安憩在
你诗集的的书页里,
一片片相依
窃窃私语着丛林的故事。

English poets | 英文诗人

From Canada | 来自加拿大

A.F. Moritz is the 6th Poet Laureate of Toronto. His most recent books are *As Far As You Know* (2020) and *The Sparrow: Selected Poems* (2018), both from House of Anansi Press. In 2015, Princeton University Press republished his 1986 volume in the Princeton Series of Contemporary Poets, *The Tradition*. He has published nineteen books of poems, and several volumes of poetry translated from French and Spanish. His poetry has received the Griffin Poetry Prize, the Guggenheim Fellowship, the Award in Literature of the American Academy of Arts and Letters, the Beth Hokin Prize of *Poetry* magazine, and other awards.

Alice Major's 11th poetry collection is *Welcome to the Anthropocene*, published by the University of Alberta Press. Science has been a source of inspiration for much of her work, including an award-winning collection of essays: *Intersecting Sets: A Poet Looks at Science*. She served as the first poet laureate for her home city of Edmonton, and her honours include an honorary doctorate of letters from the University of Alberta.

Allan Briesmaster has been active in the Toronto area literary scene since the 1980s as a workshop leader, reading series organizer, editor, and publisher. The author of eight full-length books of poetry and eight shorter books, he has given readings and talks and hosted poetry events at venues across Canada. His most recent book is *The Long Bond: Selected and New Poems* (Guernica Editions, 2019).

Bruce Hunter is the author of six books, including the novel, *In the Bear's House*, 2009 winner of the Canadian Rockies Prize at the Banff Mountain Film and Book Festival. His *Two O'clock*

Creek — Poems New and Selected won the 2010 Acorn-Plantos People's Poetry Award. In 2017, he was the Calgary Public Library's 30th Anniversary Author in Residence. In 2019, the third edition of his 1996 collection of gothic stories, *Country Music Country,* was "rebooted" with an introduction by literary historian Shaun Hunter.

Bruce Meyer is author or editor of sixty-four books of poetry, short fiction, flash fiction, non-fiction, and literary journalism. He was winner of the 2019 Freefall Prize for Poetry and the 2019 Anton Chekhov Prize for Short Fiction (UK). His most recent book of poetry is *McLuhan's Canary* (Guernica Editions, 2019) and a book of his flash fiction, *Down in the Ground* (Guernica Editions), was published in 2020.

Catherine Graham is the author of seven acclaimed poetry collections, including *The Celery Forest,* a CBC Best Book of the Year and *Aether: an out-of-body lyric.* Her award-winning debut novel *Quarry* was published in 2017. While living in Northern Ireland, Graham completed an MA in Creative Writing from Lancaster University. Winner of TIFA's Poetry *NOW* "Battle of the Bards," she teaches creative writing at the University of Toronto.

D.C. Reid's eighth book of poems, *These Elegies,* was published in 2019, and he is working on his memoir, *A Man and His River,* along with *Translated and New Poems,* featuring also the translators of his poems. His most recent awards are: the national Roderick Haig-Brown Award for sustained environmental writing, and the Somewhere My Love Poetry Anthology award.

Gerry Mattia is an author, poet and screenwriter, writing poetry since 1978. He won several awards and has adjudicated all 15 "Mattia International Poetry Competitions." In 2016, Gerry sold his first feature film screenplay.

George Elliott Clarke was the 4th Poet Laureate of Toronto and the 7th Parliamentary/Canadian Poet Laureate. He is a revered artist in song, drama, fiction, screenplay, essays, and poetry, and also a pioneering scholar of African-Canadian literature. He has taught at Duke, McGill, British Columbia, and Harvard Universities. He has won many awards, including the Governor-General's Award for Poetry, the National Magazine Gold Award for Poetry, and received the Order of Canada. Clarke has three poetry collections in Chinese, Italian, and Romanian translation.

I.B. (Bunny) Iskov is the Founder of The Ontario Poetry Society. In 2009, Bunny won the Recognizing Arts Vaughan Excellence award as an Art Educator / Mentor in the Literary Arts discipline. Her poetry has been published in several literary journals and anthologies and she has won several poetry contest prizes.

James Deahl is the author of twenty-eight literary titles, three of them from Guernica Editions: *Travelling The Lost Highway*, *Red Haws To Light The Field*, and *Rooms The Wind Makes*. In 2018, Deahl edited *Tamaracks: Canadian poetry for the 21ˢᵗ century*. He lives in Sarnia, Ontario, with the writer Norma West Linder. He is the father of Sarah, Simone, and Shona, with whom he is translating a "selected poems" of the 19ᵗʰ century Québécois poet Émile Nelligan.

Joseph Rosenblatt (1933-2019) was a long-established Canadian poet. He has won Canada's Governor-General's Award and British Columbia's B.C. Book Prize for poetry.

John B. Lee was appointed Poet Laureate of the city of Brantford in 2004 and Poet Laureate of Norfolk County in 2014. His most recent books include *Beautiful Stupid: Selected poems 2001-2018* (Black Moss Press, 2018), *This Is How We See the World* (Hidden Brook Press, 2018), and *Into a Land of Strangers* (Mosaic Press, 2019).

Kate Marshall Flaherty's sixth book of poetry, *Radiant* was launched in 2019 with Inanna Press. She was shortlisted for Arc's Poem of the Year 2019, and for Exile's Gwendolyn MacEwen Poetry Prize 2018, and won the 2018 King Foundation Georgian Bay Project Award. She has been published in *Vallum*, *Malahat Review*, *CV2*, *Grain*, *Saranac Review* etc, and was shortlisted for Descant's Best Canadian Poem, the Pablo Neruda Poetry Prize etc.

She was Toronto Rep. for the League of Canadian Poets 2012-2018. She guides StillPoint Writing Workshops and others.

Kateri Lanthier has been widely published in journals and anthologies, including *Arc*, *Green Mountains Review*, and *Best Canadian Poetry*. She won the 2013 Walrus Poetry Prize. She is an Adjunct Professor, University of Toronto. Her books are *Reporting from Night* (Iguana, 2011) and *Siren* (Véhicule Press, 2017), longlisted for the Pat Lowther Award.

Laura Lush has published four collections of poetry, a book of fiction, and a book of creative non-fiction. She is an award winning poet who lives in Guelph, Ontario and teaches creative writing in the School of Continuing Studies at the University of Toronto.

Laurence Hutchman, poet laureate of Emery, has published twelve books of poems, co-edited *Coastlines: The Poetry of Atlantic Canada* and edited *In the Writers' Words*. His collected poems *Swimming Toward the Sun* was published in 2020 by Guernica Editions. In 2007 he received the Alden Nowlan Award for Excellence. In 2001 and 2002 he taught English at the Beijing Concord College of Sino-Canada. His poems have been translated into French, Spanish, Dutch, Italian, Polish etc.

Marty Gervais is a poet, award-winning journalist, professor and publisher of one of the oldest Canadian literary presses. He was also first poet laureate for Windsor, and is the author of the Canadian bestseller *The Rumrunners*.

Meaghan Strimas is the author of three poetry collections, *Junkman's Daughter*, *A Good Time Had By All*, and *Yes or Nope*, which won the Trillium Book Award for Poetry. The editor of *The Selected Gwendolyn MacEwen*, she grew up in Owen Sound, Ontario, and lives in Toronto, where she is a professor and program coordinator at Humber College and the editor of the *Humber Literary Review*. Strimas and Priscila Uppal co-edited the *Another Dysfunctional Cancer Poem* anthology.

Milton Acorn (1923-1986), acclaimed "The People's Poet" by his peers, was a renowned Canadian poet, writer, and playwright.

Molly Peacock's latest poetry collections are *The Analyst* and *Cornucopia: New and Selected Poems*. She is the series founder of *The Best Canadian Poetry* and the co-founder of *Poetry in Motion* on New York's subways and buses. Her poems appear in leading literary journals such as *Poetry*, *The Malahat Review* and *The Hudson Review*, and are anthologized in *The Oxford Book of American Poetry*. Author of a one-person play about poetry, *The Shimmering Verge*, she is working on *Form with Feeling*, a collection of essays.

Patricia Kathleen "P. K." Page (1916-2010) was a renowned Canadian author, poet and artist with thirty books of poetry, fiction, travel diaries, and essays etc. She won many awards including the Governor General's Award and was an Officer of the Order of Canada.

Priscila Uppal (1974-2018) was a Canadian poet, novelist & playwright. Her book of poetry *Ontological Necessities* was shortlisted for the Griffin Poetry Prize. Her memoir *Projection: Encounters with My Runaway Mother* was shortlisted for the Hilary Weston Writers' Trust Prize for Nonfiction in 2013. She was also the Olympic poet-in-residence at the 2010 Vancouver Winter Games and the 2012 London Summer Games.

Patrick Connors' first chapbook, *Scarborough Songs*, was published in 2013. He was literary juror of Big Art Book 2013. His poetry was on *The Toronto Quarterly*, *This Place Anthology*, *Northern Voices Journal*, *Poetry'Z Own Magazine*, *Lummox 6 Anthology*, and was nominated for the 2011 Best of the Net contest. His recent work appeared in: *Canadian Stories*; *Big Pond Rumours*; *Sharing Spaces etc.* He is a manager for the Toronto chapter of 100,000 Poets for Change.

Richard Greene is the author of four books of poetry. His collection *Boxing the Compass* received the Governor General's Literary Award in 2010. His most recent collection, *Dante's House* was published in 2013 and was highly praised by reviewers, including George Elliott Clarke who referred to it as "a masterpiece." He is also a well-known biographer, critic, and editor.

Ronna Bloom is the author of six books of poetry. Her most recent book, *The More*, was published by Pedlar Press in 2017 and long listed for the City of Toronto Book Award. Her poems have been recorded by the CNIB and translated into Spanish, Bangla, and Chinese. She developed the first poet in residence program at Sinai Health and is currently Poet in Community at the University of Toronto. She runs workshops and gives talks on poetry, spontaneity, and awareness through writing.

Susan McMaster's publications include books, anthologies, and scripts, recordings, and collaborations with artists, dancers, dramatists, and composers. Recent collections are *Haunt* and *Lizard Love: Artists Scan Poems*. She is the founding editor of Canada's first feminist magazine, *Branching Out*, and of *Vernissage*, the magazine of the National Gallery of Canada. She is a past president of the League of Canadian Poets.

From the U.S. and elsewhere / 来自美国和其他国度

Sir Andrew Motion is an English poet, novelist, and biographer, who was Poet Laureate of the United Kingdom from 1999 to 2009. He founded the Poetry Archive. Now he lives in the U.S.A.

A.E. Stallings is the author of four poetry collections, most recently *Like*, with Farrar, Straus & Giroux. She has translated Lucretius' philosophical epic, *The Nature of Things*, and Hesiod's almanac, *Works and Days* for Penguin Classics. Awarded fellowships from the MacArthur and Guggenheim foundations, she lives in Athens, Greece.

C.D. Wright (1949-2016) was a renowned American poet. She was a MacArthur Fellow, a Guggenheim Fellow, and the Poet Laureate of Rhode Island.

Cally Conan-Davies lives by the Southern Ocean.

Dana Gioia is California's Poet Laureate. His five poetry collections include *Interrogations at Noon* (2001), which won the American Book Award, and *99 Poems: New & Selected* (2016), which won the Poets' Prize. One of his three critical collections *Can Poetry Matter?* (1992) was a finalist for the National Book Critics Award. Gioia has written four opera libretti and edited twenty literary anthologies. He served as Chairman of the National Endowment for the Arts (2003-2009) and has created the largest federal art programs in American history.

David Mason is an American writer living in Tasmania and the former poet laureate of Colorado. His latest books are *Voices, Places: Essays* and *The Sound: New and Selected Poems.*

Don Schaeffer has published a dozen poetry books such as *Until I got to New York, A Frozen Dance: Paintings and Drawings etc.*

Lois P. Jones has work published or forthcoming in *Narrative, American Poetry Journal, Tupelo Quarterly, Verse Daily, Vallentine Mitchell of London* and *Guernica Editions.* She was a winning finalist in the 2018 Terrain contest judged by Jane Hirshfield and won the Lascaux Poetry Prize, the Bristol Poetry Prize judged by Liz Berry and the Tiferet Poetry Prize. Lois hosts KPFK's Poets Café and is poetry editor of Kyoto Journal. Her book *Night Ladder* was *Glass Lyre Press*'s 2017 Editor's Choice.

Joseph Fasano is the author *The Crossing* (Cider Press Review, 2018); *Vincent* (2015); *Inheritance* (2014); and *Fugue for Other Hands* (2013), which won the Cider Press Review Book Award and was nominated for the Poets' Prize, "awarded annually for the best book of verse published by a living American poet two years prior to the award." A winner of the RATTLE Poetry Prize, among other honors, he teaches at Columbia University and Manhattanville College.

Nikki Giovanni is one of America's foremost poets. She has published numerous collections of poetry and several works of nonfiction and children's literature, and multiple recordings, including the Emmy-award nominated *The Nikki Giovanni Poetry Collection* (2004). Giovanni has taught at Rutgers University, Ohio State University, and Virginia Tech, where she is a University Distinguished Professor.

R.S. Gwynn has published six collections of verse and has edited a number of anthologies. He is a retired professor of English at Lamar University.

Rebecca Foust's recent books include *The Unexploded Ordnance Bin* (Swan Scythe Press Chapbook Award) and *Paradise Drive* (Press 53 Poetry Award), reviewed in the *Times Literary Supplement*. Recognitions include the CP Cavafy and James Hearst poetry prizes, the Lascaux and *American Literary Review* fiction prizes, the Constance Rooke Creative Nonfiction Prize, and fellowships from The Frost Place, Hedgebrook, MacDowell, and Sewanee. Foust was Marin County Poet Laureate in 2017-19 and works as Poetry Editor for *Women's Voices for Change*, an assistant Editor for *Narrative Magazine* and co-producer of a new series about poetry for Marin TV, *Rising Voices*.

来自华语诗人 | From Chinese poets

洛夫 (1928-2018) 台湾现代诗杰出诗人，生于中国湖南，1954年与张默、痖弦创办《创世纪》诗刊，历任总编辑多年。著有37部诗集，作品被译成英、法、日、韩、荷兰、瑞典等文，有诗魔之称。代表作《石室之死亡》《时间之伤》《漂木》等。

痖弦台湾重要诗人，1954年与张默、洛夫共同创办《创世纪》诗刊。痖弦以诗之开创和拓植知名，民谣写实与心灵探索之风格体会，五十年来蔚为现代诗大家，从之者既众，影响最为深远，出版有《痖弦诗集》《中国新诗研究》《记哈客诗想》《聚散花序Ⅰ》等书。

辛牧(1943-)台湾人,目前担任创世纪诗杂志总编辑。曾获：优秀青年诗人奖、台北市捷运公车诗文征选新诗首奖、文艺奖章—文学创作奖、2015年WCP第35届世界诗人大会桂冠诗人奖。已出版诗集：散落的树羽、辛牧诗选、辛牧短诗选〈中英对照〉、蓝白拖、问鱼。

古月，本名胡玉衡，湖南衡山人。曾获中国文艺学会优秀青年诗人奖。诗集：《追随太阳步伐的人》《月之祭》《我爱》《浮生》/《探月》《巡花筑梦》等。散文集：《诱惑者》。传记：《革命先烈——吴禄贞传》，青少年历史读物《北方之雄——吴禄贞》等。

肖今，原名金国青，浙江人，出生于1977年。2003年开始创作，作品散见于《台湾新闻报》、《文汇报》、《上海诗人》、《澳洲彩虹鹦》、《浙江作家》等刊物，作有长诗《乱码》、《MISSING》。

蓝蓝 (1967—) 生于中国山东。出版有十多部诗集：《含笑终生》《内心生活》《从这里，到这里》《唱吧，悲伤》《世界的渡口》《从缪斯山谷归来》；中英文双语诗集《身体里的峡谷》、《钉子》；俄语诗集《歌声之杯》；童诗集《诗人与小树》以及散文随笔集六部，童话集五部等。获第四届诗歌与人国际诗人奖、冰心儿童文学新作奖、中国新世纪女诗人十佳、第三届袁可嘉诗歌奖、第四届维拉国际年度艺术家奖等

李少君1967年生，湖南人，著有《自然集》《草根集》《海天集》、《神降临的小站》等，被誉为"自然诗人"。曾任《天涯》杂志主编，海南省作协副主席，现为中国作家协会《诗刊》社副主编。

沈河（1963—2008）作品发表在《人民文学》、《诗刊》、《星星》等。曾获《人民文学》《诗刊》诗歌等级奖。

李加建，1935年出生在四川。出版有诗集、长篇小说、短篇小说集、杂文集、随笔记等多种。现为自由撰稿人。

高梁生于1966年中国河北。出版诗集《秘境》，多次获国内几种诗歌奖

何均：作品发表在海内外报刊,著有诗集《明镜集》《清晨，我遭遇必然的蝴蝶》，小说集《伍镇》，散文集《真意》，《何均作品选》

杯中冲浪，本名王旭胜，山东人，1965年出生。中学教师。曾出版诗集《鸟和鸟巢》。

大卫树：2004年加盟酷我北美枫文学论坛，任版主和驻站作家。曾出版诗集《卍经：五千年第一诗》和《花瓣诗》。

李广田（1906~1968）中国优秀诗人散文作家，先后结集的还有《雀蓑集》、《圈外》、《回声》、《日边随笔》等。

林静，旅美詩人、書法家、新文學社社長，現居紐約。1973年出生。2006年創辦《新文學》雜誌並擔任主編，現兼任世界書畫家聯合會及國際音樂交流協會藝術顧問。

蔡利华，中国重庆人，诗人、作家、高级工程师、大学客座教授。著有诗集《重金属的梦魇》《今天是明天的佐料》，散文集《回首蓦见》，短篇小说集《边缘地带》，文论集《诗语人生》。

晓鸣，中国四川人，曾任北美中西文化交流协会会长。1981年开始发表诗歌，小说和散文。

阿九，诗人，翻译家和环境工程师。他的第一本诗歌著

作《语言》于2012年出版。他获得了PEW-DJS诗歌翻译奖（2015年）和获得性文学翻译奖（2018年）。他的《菲利普·拉金诗歌全集》的中文译本被《新京报》选为2018年10本最佳书籍之一。

天端，杭州人，诗人和化学博士。现居美国。中国诗歌学会会员。主编《诗行天下—中国当代海外学子诗词集》《天涯诗路——中国当代海外诗人作品荟萃》《海内外当代诗词选》，主编《海外诗库》。

姚园，重庆人。现居美国西雅图，美国《常青藤》诗刊主编。曾获全球征文比赛一等奖、第三届中国最佳诗歌编辑奖、丝绸之路国际诗歌艺术金奖等。在海内外出版社出版有十余本文学书籍。

ABOUT THE TRANSLATOR | 译者介绍

Anna Yin was Mississauga's Inaugural Poet Laureate. She was born in Hunan, China, and immigrated to Canada in 1999. Anna has authored six poetry books and won awards, including the 2005 Ted Plantos Memorial Award, 2010/2014 MARTYs, 2013 Professional Achievement Award from CPAC (Cross-Cultural Professionals Association of Canada), 2016/2017 scholarships from West Chester University Poetry Conference and three grants from the Ontario Arts Council. Her poems in English & Chinese and ten translations by her appear in a Canadian Studies textbook used by Humber College. Her poems have been published in ARC Poetry, New York Times, CBC, World Journal, China Daily, etc. Her reading and Poetry Alive workshops were featured at several International Poetry Festivals.

website: annapoetry.com

星子安娜（Anna Yin)加拿大密西沙加市首任桂冠诗人，生于中国湖南，99年移民加拿大。著有四本英文诗集和双语诗集《爱的灯塔》，中英文作品在中国日报，纽约时报，世界日报，加拿大文学评论，世界诗歌等刊物发表。安娜荣获2005年安省的Ted Plantos 纪念奖，2010/2014 MARTY文学奖，2013加拿大中国专业人士协会的专业成就奖以及2016/2017年西切斯特大学诗歌大会奖学金和三个安省艺术协会文学项目奖。安娜作品和翻译作品被选入加拿大HUMBER学院国际留学生班的教材，国家诗歌月等项目。她多次受邀在国际诗歌节上诗歌表演和举办讲座。

ACKNOWLEDGEMENTS | 鸣谢

Many translations in this collection have been published by the following magazines, thanks to their editors. Also speciel thanks to all the contributors for permission to reprint the original. 此书中很多翻译获得以下刊物发表，衷心感谢：

Yidan Han: 《詩天空》 | *Poetry Sky*
Coviews Editors: 《北美枫》 | *North American Maple*
Warner Tchan: 《新大陆诗刊 》 | *New World Poetry*
Canadian Editors: *Room Magazine*
Mindy: 《诗东西》 | *Poetry East West*
Yao yuan: 《常青藤诗刊》 | *IVY Poetry*
Lin Jing: 《新文学》 | *New Literature*

（也衷心感谢所有诗人的授权收录原作发表）

Special thanks to Terry Barker and Allan Briesmaster for checking the English part, A Jiu, Mindy, Xiao Ming, Qi Liang, Wen Zhang and Leslie Yang for checking my translations. They have provided me valuable suggestions and insights. I am also grateful for my family's support. Thank you all for believing in "Mirrors and Windows". Finally I want to thank Guernica Editions and Michael Mirolla for publishing this book.

特别感谢特雷·巴克和艾伦·贝瑞斯马斯特校对英文部分，明迪，晓鸣，慕亮，张雯，杨律检查我的翻译. 感谢大家为我提供了宝贵的建议和见解。我也很感谢家人的支持。感谢大家相信"镜子和窗户"。最后我要衷心感谢Guernica Editions 和Michael Mirolla出版这本书。